Singapore: Malaysia: Brunei

Singapore: Malaysia: Brunei

John Cockcroft

Angus and Robertson

Contents

First published in 1971 by
ANGUS & ROBERTSON LTD

221 George Street, Sydney
107 Elizabeth Street, Melbourne
89 Anson Road, Singapore
54 Bartholomew Close, London

ISBN 0 207 12036 6
© John Cockcroft 1970

Registered in Australia for
transmission by post as a book

PRINTED IN HONG KONG

The island of Singapore

Flying into Singapore, the gateway to Asia, is a unique experience. Below the aircraft ships lay at anchorage in Keppel Harbour, tied up bow to stern along the 23 miles of wharves. In between the large foreign-going vessels at anchor, tiny sampans, tong-kangs and junks were making their way into Singapore, loaded with goods from all points of the compass—Thailand, Borneo, Sumatra—their brown sails billowing and straining to get into port. The large eyes painted on the prows to stave off evil spirits searched for the quickest way into harbour and then to the Singapore River. The white-wash of the bows, the blue sea, the yellows, whites and reds of the larger vessels with their colours of many nations flying at the mast-heads, gave a clean, washed look. The fresh north-east monsoon rippled the surface of the harbour, and as we came in closer to shore the water turned from blue to a muddy brown, with flotsam and jetsam from a thousand ports.

On the mainland of Singapore Island, the towering buildings of Queenstown came into view: thousands of pieces of washing hanging from poles on the balconies fluttered and waved in a colourful array—like so many flags of welcome. Across the city the traffic flowed in chaotic fashion under a haze of burnt gasoline.

I have always been fascinated by Singapore from the time when I visited the place as a child—the very name has always had an air of romance and mystery. Today it is a dynamic, fast developing nation, soon to become an industrial giant of South-east Asia. The people of these 224 square miles of island have a purpose—a determination to weld their multi-racial society into a nation that wants to get on with the job of living.

Singapore is China, India, Europe, Malaysia—all wrapped into one. It is the world's fourth largest port, and its principal market for rubber, tin and pepper. Nowhere else—with the exception of Malaysia—does east meet west so fully. Chinese, Ceylonese, Indians, Pakistanis, Arabs, Filipinos, Malays, Indonesians, Eurasians, Europeans, and Hindus, Christians, Confucians, Buddhists, Jews, Taoists and Muslims live side by side and work together.

THE TROPICAL HARBOUR AT NIGHT

For the visitor to Singapore there is so much to see. Where does he start? My first evening was spent with the *Singapore Lady*, a restaurant floating in the harbour. I arrived at Collyer Quay in the centre of the city at 6.30 p.m.—at that stage of the evening when the lights cast a pleasant glow over the city and the ships in Keppel Harbour. The canopy of reds, blues and golds in the sky gave the whole dock-side area a different atmosphere. Darkness fell quickly, as it always does in the tropics and a cold artificial light was left illuminating the scene.

At the quay steps I boarded a catamaran with red curtains hanging from the orange roof that sheltered comfortable seats. In a few moments the motor started and

5

we made our way round the bows and sterns of vessels at anchor. Some towered above us empty of cargo, others floated deep, waiting to be unloaded—fat, bloated creatures of the night. We slowed down and pulled in alongside the *Singapore Lady*. The motor stopped, and across the huge stretch of harbour came voices of seamen speaking in the many languages of the world, the noise of the traffic on shore and the chugging of the lighters coming and going with cargo from the ships, each struggling to drown out other sounds. This is a world of its own, where work never stops.

Climbing from the catamaran I walked through a beautifully appointed foyer into the Islander Room. Upstairs is the Malacca Room, and above that the Sunset Deck. The restaurant has furnishings and decorations from all parts of Asia: chairs from Thailand, pearlshell from the Philippines, urns from Persia. Hanging on the ceiling of the main deck are electrically driven punkahs—fans about two feet long made of cloth on a frame. They sway backwards and forwards to make a most effective room-cooler.

After dinner, I walked with my host up to the Sunset Deck and looked across to the outskirts of the harbour, as we cruised along at a steady pace. In the darkness, and not too far away, the black humps of the Rhio Islands loomed on the horizon. To the north lay Vietnam and to the south and under the same stars, Sumatra; to the east, Borneo. Sliding peacefully along the black waters, we turned to go back to Singapore, when a large black sampan came out of the darkness, its white eyes piercing the gloom. The sampan swished past us, and behind it the rich odours of the spices, the rubber, the copra, and other smells of the East hung in the air.

Across on the shore the lights of Singapore blazed. The *Singapore Lady* slowed down and stopped. I made my way back to Collyer Quay, thinking I had been looking at once into the past, present and future of Asia.

On the way to the Goodwood Park Hotel we passed along Orchard Road, where each evening brings a change of scene. In the daytime, parked cars fill a large stretch of concrete which forms part of the street. At dusk the cars disappear and portable food stalls come out to take their place. Each of these portable cafes has its own tables, and its own array of food. Bright lights are strung above and flames fly from grillers as steaks or chickens are cooked to the customer's liking. People wander in and out from early evening till early morning. At daylight the concrete is bare once more, waiting for the rumble of approaching vehicles.

THE HEART OF SINGAPORE

Singapore is dynamic. It jingles and jangles, swings and sways, and everybody works on this tiny island. The people may be of many races and creeds, but together they are Singaporeans.

One of the most interesting places to explore is Chinatown, where streets and alleys are filled with the noise of a dozen dialects and the smell of oriental spices. Here the gourmet can sample Hokkien, Cantonese, or Teochew dishes in dozens of tiny food shops. The many Chinese temples are centres of noisy and colourful ritual; processions with fire crackers, clashing cymbals and brass bands celebrate the birthday of a god, or the funeral of a wealthy citizen.

Between Collyer Quay and Raffles Place is Change Alley, a lively little shopping arcade crowded with stalls and a great deal of activity. Visitors wander from stall to stall comparing prices amid the persuasive chatter of vendors, each offering a better bargain than the next. I asked a Chinese friend to bargain for a cigarette lighter: she settled for nine dollars, but I bought the same lighter for seven at another stall. Everyone bargains—it is an accepted custom in Singapore. People will even bargain for a handful of rice. I saw a visitor buying the same cigarette lighter for eleven dollars and looking very pleased.

6

I walked down Sago Street past Pagoda, Temple, Mosque and Chin Chew streets, all crowded, all noisy. Wending my way through the crowds I noticed large stalls heavily laden with oranges from Australia. Behind these, out of the sun, sat the calligrapher, writing Chinese characters in gold on red pieces of paper. The calligrapher plays an important part in Chinese life; he writes letters and religious texts for those who require them. This particular calligrapher, slightly built with kindly features, wore steel-framed glasses. He sat at a small wooden table in front of his house, hidden from view by a piece of hanging canvas. Along the wall above his table hung numerous red paper pennants with delicately drawn Chinese characters in black, silver and gold. On his table he had packets of airmail envelopes, writing paper, a stack of red paper, ink and brushes.

The calligrapher could not speak English and I could not speak Chinese, and after a short session of head nodding and hand waving, trying to convey the impression that I wanted to take his picture, I realized we were getting nowhere. Then his married daughter arrived. She spoke English to me and rapid Cantonese to her father, and everything was arranged in no time. After taking the pictures of the calligrapher and his daughter with her chubby infant, I pushed aside the hanging canvas and wandered down Sago Street, passing the many stalls displaying bright yellow fruits, cakes, biscuits and the crisp pastry for which the Chinese cooks are renowned. A juice-seller stood busily crushing sugar-cane and making drinks.

Round the next corner the scene became more lively. Here at the fish market, people were selling turtles, and fish of all kinds. Snakes, too, were skinned and sold.

I noticed the women in their Cheong Sams, the one-piece costume that buttons up to the neck and has a long slit in the side seam of the skirt. Other women wore the pyjama-like suit called the Sam Foo. Children could be seen at work—those who were not at school at this time of day.

Above me as I walked faces watched from windows, behind long poles of fluttering garments drying in the sun. I gave a nod of my head and a broad wink and the faces smiled. From everywhere rose the incessant babble of several Chinese languages; in the distance, the constant blare of car horns. Occasionally someone spoke to me in English, asking if I would like some snake or other delicacy to take home, and smiling at my reaction.

A Chinese funeral: After strolling round the stalls and crossing streets I eventually found myself in Sago Lane among the death houses and coffin makers. A Chinese funeral had just begun, accompanied by a band playing loudly. At the head of the procession moved a large decorated truck, its blue banners lettered with white Chinese characters and surrounded by rosettes of flowers. On the tray of the truck lay the coffin covered with green leaves, orchids and frangipani.

Immediately behind the coffin came the principal mourner, probably the eldest son of the deceased. Women followed on foot, dressed in ankle-length, white wrap-arounds with white sashes. On their heads they wore peaked hats that hung down the back to waist level, where the ends were tied with the sash.

Then came two men carrying a replica of the blue banner; behind them two cymbal players, two cornet players and a drummer, followed by the professional mourners. The funeral party moved out of Chinatown to the noise of fire-crackers and the clashing of cymbals.

All this is part of the daily picture, business going on just the same. A street seller continued to stack his towels, face washers, soaps and powders on the pieces of timber he had laid on the street, and across the road the juice vendor still crushed sugar-cane for the sweet drinks he sold to the passing crowd.

The temple medium: From Chinatown I travelled westward to Bukit Purmei Road, to the temple of Soon Thiam Keng. This is a difficult place to find; the car had to be parked precariously on the side of the road, leaving just enough room for one car to pass at a time. I walked up some steps, along a path and arrived at the top of the hill at the Monkey God Temple, the name by which it is generally known. Thirteen hundred years ago the Chinese Buddhist Hsuan Tsuang travelled from China to India to collect religious literature to take back to China. Hsuan Tsuang took twelve years to make his round journey and during that time the monkeys befriended and helped him. The Monkey God, presumed to be Hanuman of the Ramayana epic, is worshipped by some of the Chinese.

Behind the temple lives the medium—a young man, slight in build and alert. He came over and introduced himself in excellent English, adding "If you want any close-up pictures, let me know". He told me of his work as a medium—how he acts as a communicator between the devotee and the Monkey God. The Chinese believe in the spirits of their ancestors and practise ancestor worship. The medium attempts to communicate with the spirits and the gods, and endeavours to solve the problems of the devotees. Some problems require drastic solutions, such as cutting the tongue, the stomach or back with a knife. On the 16th day of the 8th moon, when the birthday of the Monkey God is celebrated, the medium strikes and slashes himself with a fearsome-looking instrument—a round iron ball about four inches in diameter with dozens of iron spikes, about five or six inches long, projecting from it.

Women at work: The visitor to Singapore is always fascinated by the Sam Sui women who work on the roads or on new buildings. These women are easily recognized by the blue pants and blouse they wear and the red scarf folded round their heads. The Sam Sui originally came from Southern China and belong to a matriarchal group. If a Sam Sui woman marries, her husband stays at home to look after the children. Usually, they do not marry, but remain a celibate group, living together and pooling their resources. As workers they are unsurpassed, yet it is strange to see them working on scaffolds of high buildings, on roads, or hillsides.

The backstop of every family in Singapore is the Amah, who serves as a paid cook, nursemaid and housekeeper. She wears a uniform of black pants and a white blouse. Some of these women, too, remain celibate, and young Amahs ("nieces") are adopted by older ones ("aunties"). The nieces look after the old aunties who are no longer able to work.

8

COLOUR

Hand-carved and painted with gold, this wooden ornament is part of the 300-years-old Chinese temple at Malacca

Market places stretched along the sides of streets are part of the everyday scene in Singapore and Malaysia

The sugar-cane seller is a popular part of the life of Singapore—a land of perpetual summer

Batik painting by Penang artist Yong Cheng Wah, of a kind gaining wide recognition in the world today

Festivals and entertainments: Festivals are many on this cosmopolitan island. The Chinese celebrate a noisy New Year with fire-crackers and lion dances, and festivities continue for 15 days. The Mooncake Festival reminds them of the political oppression of earlier times, when secret messages were hidden in cakes to evade the tyrannical rule of Mongol overlords.

Hindu houses glow with oil candles during the Festival of Lights, the *Deepavali*, which commemorates the slaying of a mythical tyrant king. The *Thaipusam* is a display of Hindu religious fervour. Processions of worshippers crowd the streets— some with steel skewers driven into their bodies as penance for their sins. The temple deity is paraded through the streets on a decorated chariot, and there is fire-walking in the temples.

The Muslims, too, have their festival days. The *Hari Raya Puasa*, the first day of the tenth month in the Mohammedan calendar, marks the end of the *Bulan Puasa*, or fasting month. At this time the streets of Singapore are alive with colour: the Malays come out in their gay and elaborate national costumes, and decorate their homes with lights and banners. All muslims commence this day with ceremonial ablutions, and like to visit parents and religious teachers before mosque to seek blessing and forgiveness for any wrongs they may have committed in the past year.

The visitor to Singapore can find much to entertain him. At the Villa Saujana dancers in lavish batik and silk costumes revive the old Malay art that once pleased the courtiers of the Sri Vijaya and Majapahit empires. Many folk dances tell simple stories of love and daily toils—the Malayan Rice Harvest Dance has been performed ever since rice was first harvested. The Villa Saujana also gives exhibitions of the skilful though dangerous *bersilat*—the Malayan art of self-defence.

In the fashionable district of Tanglin are Singapore's Botanic Gardens, where jungle trees are hung with lianas, and monkeys run wild through the foliage. Winding paths lead to a miniature lake and pavilion, and to a plant house containing a rare collection of orchids.

I travelled a little way out of Singapore City to spend an hour viewing Johnnie Johnson's world-famous shell collection—one of the largest in the world, with over 2,500 shells.

Nights in Singapore may be spent shopping in the neon-lit stalls of the Pasar Malam (the nomadic night market found in a different part of the city each week); at a Chinese opera or variety show at the National Theatre; watching Indian dancers in a cabaret, or sampling rich foods at one of the dozens of excellent Indian, Malay, Chinese or continental restaurants.

I have travelled much in the East, yet it still seems incredible that just five hours from Sydney with an airline such as Qantas (a little longer from London or New York) brings me to the great variety of life in Singapore and the mainland of Asia.

GOVERNMENT AND CONSTITUTION

Singapore is divorced politically from Malaysia. It became an independent and sovereign republic within the British Commonwealth on 9th August, 1965, having been a member of the Federation of Malaysia since 16th September, 1963. The Republic celebrates its national day on 9th August, the anniversary of separation from Malaysia. On 21st September, 1965, Singapore was elected the 117th member of the United Nations.

The Republic has a parliamentary system of government based on full adult suffrage. Fifty-eight members from one-member constituencies are elected by secret ballot, for a maximum of five years. Head of State is the President, elected by parliament for a period of four years; President Yusof bin Ishak was elected in 1967 for a third term.

13

The Prime Minister is appointed by the President: he must be a member of parliament and have the support of the majority of his party members. The ten cabinet ministers are appointed by the President on the advice of the Prime Minister.

Parliament is presided over by a Speaker, and debates may be conducted in any or all of the official languages: Malay, Mandarin, Tamil and English.

For reasons of economy and efficiency there are no local government bodies; the former City Council and Rural Board have been taken over by Government departments. Judicial power is in the hands of a Court of Appeal and a High Court, consisting of a Chief Justice and six judges.

In 1959 Lee Kuan Yew became Prime Minister of Singapore and with him came self-government, but real independence was not achieved till the separation from Malaysia in 1965.

After 1959 dynamic progress was made in many fields—in housing, education, health and industry. The new consciousness of being Singaporeans inspired an already hard-working and enthusiastic people, and so did the brilliant and confident leadership of Lee Kuan Yew. Planning, building, and expansion continue at an astonishing rate; everywhere changes are rapid, and of a kind that will benefit an integrated nation.

The housing explosion: Since Sir Stamford Raffles's landing in 1819 the population has grown from 200 to 2,000,000. Immigrants poured in and overcrowding turned many areas into slums; but the old shophouses with 16 families to a kitchen are becoming a thing of the past since the Housing and Development Board began building multi-storey flats on the outskirts of the city. In 1965, at the end of the first five-year, low cost housing plan, 54,000 flats had gone up. Queenstown became the first of Singapore's satellite towns—with 36,000 units.

Much of the money to finance the buildings comes from the people themselves. Health and life insurance premiums are paid into a Central Provident Fund which is then reinvested by the Government in local housing. The rent paid by tenants—about $S60 a month for a three-roomed flat—helps to keep finance circulating. Many contributors to the Central Provident Fund can afford to buy their apartments, either outright, or on time-payment over a period of up to 15 years.

TRADE AND SHIPPING

Singaporeans have a firm belief that within a few years they will be one of the largest exporters of manufactured goods in the world. With hard work and careful planning the nation is starting new industries that will have far-reaching effects in the years to come. Today, Singapore's light manufactured goods—textiles and garments in particular—are of a quality that has surprised even the people who live there. New industries have created a vast market for raw materials such as wool and cotton, rubber, petroleum by-products and timber.

Industrial centres: At Jurong, close by, one stage of an industrial complex stretches over 17,000 acres; its steel mills, oil refinery, shipyards, and over 200 factories form a huge hive of activity. Manufactured goods include clothing, furniture, chemicals and steel and rubber products. Capital is being invested so rapidly that all the available land at Jurong is now taken up and plans are in operation to extend the area to cope with the increased demand for light and heavy industry.

The complex is completely self-contained: it has its own harbour, railway line and power supply. All the workers of the area are housed in multi-storey apartment buildings—called highrise apartments—a short distance from the factories. The apartments have their own shopping centre, dispensary, school, and whatever

14

facilities are required by their occupants. Smaller industrial estates like Redhill and Kampong Arang are engaged in light manufacturing.

The Republic also includes several small islands: Pulo Brani is a centre for tin smelting; Pulau Samboe and Blakan Mati have oil refineries and storage tanks. St Johns Island, only twelve miles from the Indonesian Rhio Islands, is a quarantine station.

Singapore imports most of her food commodities from South-east Asia, America, Europe, Australia and New Zealand. A well-constructed macadamized causeway carries road and rail traffic across the Johore Strait to the peninsula. Water is piped across this causeway from Malaysia, for the island cannot store sufficient water for industrial needs.

Agriculture: About 50 square miles of country in Singapore and the near-by islands are set aside for agriculture—mainly fruit, vegetables, coconuts and rubber. The Government has done much to increase production in rural areas by providing an advisory service on all aspects of crop cultivation and farm management. Crop pests are brought under control, and farmers are trained in new farming techniques. Poultry, eggs and pigs have become major exports.

The port of Singapore: Trade and shipping go hand in hand. I counted over 120 ships in the harbour, anchored a couple of miles out or tied up along the wharves. The Port Authority is a statutory body organized to administer the whole of the harbour—1,000 acres on shore, and 125 nautical square miles. Its members are drawn from the Government, from shipping and insurance companies, and from banks; its activities make Singapore the fourth largest port in the world. The field of administration is vast and includes every aspect of entrepôt activity—shipment and transhipment of cargo, storage in godowns (warehouses), banking, insurance, communications and the constant renovation and extension of port facilities.

The island's trade grew from the river trade of many years ago—when ships anchored mid-stream to have their cargoes loaded onto sampans and lighters, which sailed up the Singapore River. Today this is still the pattern: cargo from large vessels is transferred to lighters and taken to godowns for storage. The double-handling of cargo is gradually being eliminated as more wharf space becomes available. There are at present 30 berths for ships, of which five are for coastal shipping.

Separate areas have been allocated for containerisation, and by 1971 a whole complex for container shipping, costing nearly 76 million dollars, will be in operation. Cranes along the wharves load containers for shipment to ports throughout South-east Asia.

Along the waterfront on the way to the airport the visitor notices dozens of junks tied up or anchored offshore. These vessels are not used as much as they once were but some still carry cargo and engage in barter trade. They bring in cargo from Indonesia or other South-east Asian countries, unload their goods and reload with other goods for the return trip. Very little money, if any, changes hands at any time. The bulk of the cargo brought into Singapore is rubber, which is graded and packed, then reshipped to other countries. In return the junks receive foodstuffs for sale or exchange in the ports of pick-up.

The port of Singapore has been serving the 2,500 million people of Asia for decades. Both mainland China and nationalist China are selling a wide range of goods in Singapore. Manufactured goods, food and machinery flow in from Europe, America and Japan, for importation or distribution to the countries of South-east Asia. Australia and New Zealand also ship huge quantities of cargo through this island entrepôt.

With more than half the population under 21 years of age special emphasis has been placed on education. The Government's aim is to give every child at least ten years' education, without discrimination against race, language, sex, religion or social status.

Schools: The Ministry of Education has been building schools at the rate of one a month since 1960.

Singapore children spend six years in primary school and four to six years in secondary school; the minimum school-leaving age is 16. Examinations are held at the end of the final primary school year for entrance to secondary school. The School Certificate Examination is held at the end of the fourth year of secondary school. A pass qualifies the student for technical or teacher training, or the public service. Students who study for a further two years may then obtain the Higher School Certificate, which qualifies them for entrance to a university.

As in most countries, there are private and public schools in Singapore: the private schools generally being a commercial or religious venture without financial aid from the Government. Smaller private schools are run by foreign nationals for their own children.

Teaching is aided by the Singapore Educational Television System; programmes are arranged in accordance with the school curriculum, and telecast in several languages throughout the school year.

Primary school children have four and a half hours of school a day, secondary school children five and a half hours. Heavy class loads are broken up by dividing the school day into two shifts, so that some pupils can attend in the morning, and others in the afternoon. Each teacher works for a total of 20 hours a week. So, the children you see playing or working in the mornings go off to school at midday, and those you see at work in the afternoons started school at 7 a.m.

The universities: The foundations of the University of Singapore were laid as early as 1905 when a College of Medicine was established. Later, Raffles College was built to celebrate the centenary of the founding of the free-trade port. It took ten years to build and was opened in 1929.

Both these colleges were responsible for the higher education of a large number of students from Malaya and Singapore, as well as from northern Borneo, though some students were sent to England for secondary and tertiary education.

In World War II Raffles College closed when the Japanese occupied the building and made it their headquarters. The Medical College continued to function and during the war years the Japanese conferred degrees on successful graduates. After the war, in 1946, Raffles College reopened and in 1949 was amalgamated with the College of Medicine to become the University of Malaya. When Malaysia became independent in 1957 a branch of the University was established in Kuala Lumpur. Then, in 1961 the two branches became two separate universities, the University of Malaya in Kuala Lumpur, and the University of Singapore, which opened officially on 1st January, 1962. The University of Singapore has six faculties: science, medicine, arts, law, social science and dentistry; and two schools: the school of education and that of pharmacy. Of the students enrolled (approximately 4,000), about one third are girls. Four halls of residence accommodate 1,000 students.

The majority of the academic staff is drawn from Singapore and Malaysia, but some lecturers come from Australia, Britain, Ceylon, India, Hong Kong and the United States.

The University operates on annual budget of about $S11 million. Government

16

subsidies are large, and fees can be kept low as a result. The full course of social science, including medical insurance, costs the student about $S160, or $U.S.50 (there are approximately three Singapore dollars to the United States dollar).

Other tertiary centres of learning are the Nanyang University at Jurong, with arts, science and commerce faculties, and the Polytechnic, where diplomas in accountancy, architecture and engineering may be obtained. The Ngee Ann College, a private institution opened in 1963, has seven faculties, including Chinese and Malay languages, and business administration.

The number of university places is restricted because the work available for graduates is limited: thus, competition is keen. At the moment, all graduates can find employment, though in the field of medicine each doctor treats an average of only 1,800 patients, and it is said that there are a few too many lawyers and far too many pharmacists. (In several South-east Asian countries graduates are unable to find suitable positions.)

THE ARTS

The National Theatre Trust: Singapore is not all industry, business and sightseeing: it is a place of art, music and theatre. The National Theatre is evidence of this.

In 1963 the Government formed the National Theatre Trust and the National Theatre. The Trust manages the Theatre and does everything possible to foster and develop a national culture in Singapore. The members of the Trust include a good cross-section of the island community.

Each village in Singapore, as in Malaysia, has always had its own dramatic society—there are hundreds of these little theatre groups scattered throughout the island. The National Theatre Trust is now bringing all these groups together, and the results are proving beneficial to the nation. The facilities of the National Theatre foster contact between artists of different cultural streams, who are able to observe each other at work and exchange ideas and techniques in an intimate workshop atmosphere.

On the musical side are the National Theatre Company's three orchestras—Chinese, Indian and Malay. All are ambitious ventures, but if the National Theatre Trust has the drive that makes Singapore grow in other directions, they will be successful ones.

The Trust also sponsors a quarterly literary magazine, to be distributed internationally and provide encouragement and stimulation for Singapore poets and writers; some of these already have international reputations. While visiting Dr Goh Poh Seng, President of the National Theatre Trust, I read several of the poems published in the quarterly, *The Immigration Office*, by the poet Edwin Thumboo, begins:

> They are polite
> Perhaps uncertain if you come or go
> Or be some secret official,
> Who, provoked by even a subtle diffidence
> Of voice or gesture,
> Can summarise a promising career.
> They were polite, tentatively,
> Comprehensive too, enquiring into
> Destination, origin, intention
> Locations of your interests,
> As if they hoped to find some plan for
> Mis-adventure, or whether you were merely powerful,
> They found that I was just a citizen
> With a vote: their politeness slumped
> And sought to disengage the good intentions.

The art of batik painting: The most highly developed fields of art in Singapore are sculpture and painting; is not surprising, since it is easier for a multi-racial society to express itself in these than in any other art form, with the possible exception of the dance. Moreover, visitors have always patronized the visual arts to a greater extent, and this has also contributed to their development.

Singapore is becoming an art centre. Among the artists of international renown are the *batik* painters Seah Kim Joo of Singapore and Yong Cheng Wah, from Penang. When I visited his gallery Seah Kim Joo explained the technique of *batik* painting, which is becoming so popular. *Batik* cloth has always been used for clothing —it was not until the last few years that *batik* work has emerged as a painting technique.

The materials used are a piece of white cloth of very fine weave, on which the design is drawn, and thin wax containing bees' wax and resin, which is melted and poured into a container called a *tjanting*—a brass utensil with a small bowl and hollow tube at one end through which the wax flows.

The wax is applied to certain areas of the design, then the colour is applied to the area not covered by the wax. A brush is used for large areas, the *tjanting* for finer work. After the first coat of colour has been applied it is covered with an insulating layer of wax, and the original wax is removed from the areas where the second colour is to be applied. And so the process goes on: the wax is taken off each unpainted part, then melted and applied to the painted areas. This is time-consuming work—there can be as many as seven different applications, depending on the number of colours used.

The *batik* paintings command various prices from about $S180 to $S400, and prints sell from about $S30. Singapore and Malaysia are the only two countries specializing in this type of painting. Seah Kim Joo and Yong Cheng Wah have shown the principle of *batik* painting to artists in other countries.

18

Peoples of the region

LANDS OF MANY RACES

Living in Malaysia today are about 4,500,000 Malays, 3,250,000 Chinese, and nearly 1,000,000 Indians and Pakistanis. In Singapore live about 1,490,000 Chinese, 290,000 Malays, and 161,000 Indians and Pakistanis.

These groups make up most of the population of Malaysia, Singapore and Brunei. In addition, there are Eurasians and Europeans, as well as jungle peoples—the Senoi, Jakuns and Negritos of the Malayan peninsula, and the Kadazans, Bajaus and Muruts of Sabah. Of the many indigenous peoples of Sarawak, the Ibans, Bidayahs and Kayans are the main ones. In Brunei, where the population exceeds 120,000, Malays and Chinese predominate.

Growth of the population: The most significant increase in the population of the Malayan peninsula and Singapore occurred between the late 18th and early 20th centuries, when Chinese, Indian and Indonesian migrations took place under British rule.

Most of the Indian immigrants came to Malaya from southern India, to work on rubber plantations under the indenture system established by the Government of India in 1838. Workers were recruited on a three-year labour contract. When the term expired they were offered a free trip home, but many remained, and by the time the system was abolished in 1920, many thousands of Indians and Pakistanis had made their home on the Malayan Peninsula and in Singapore.

The Chinese had a similar arrangement before communist rule. Instead of sending their money back to China, the Chinese invested it in property and businesses in Malaysia.

At this stage, the increase among Indians and Chinese was very low, because they brought few women with them when they migrated, and the incidence of fatal tropical diseases was high. In the case of the Indonesian migrants, though the death rate was high, it was balanced by the birth rate, for men had brought their wives with them. After World War I the ratio of the sexes among Indians and Chinese became more even, and the birth rate increased. At the same time, advances in tropical medicine meant that more lives could be saved. Today, the Chinese in Singapore (many have migrated there) have one of the highest birth rates in the world—and over-population is becoming a problem for the Government of all countries of the region.

In northern Borneo the overall population increase was slower. Here again, the death rate was high. The people lived in scattered areas, and even though medical skill advanced it failed to reach many. Though the Muruts of Sarawak still have one of the lowest birth rates in the world, the population increase in Borneo has speeded up considerably since 1949 (no exact figures are available). The death rate in Sabah was nearly 14% between 1945 and 1949, and by 1960 it had dropped to 8.3%.

Merging of the peoples: In the main, the mixed races of Malaysia, Singapore and Brunei form contented communities, tolerant of the racial, cultural and religious differences of their members. In a village of 50 houses you will find Chinese, Indians—both Muslim and Hindu—and Malays. All feel they are part of the village: they visit each other and make friends, they all speak the common language—Malay, and most speak one or two other languages as well.

Malaysians are a people with a purpose: the future of their country. One of the aims of the Malaysian Government is to form and develop a policy that will bring all the ethnic groups together, making them a loyal and united people. And despite the diversity of race, language and culture, a distinctive Malaysian society is emerging, for ties of friendship and loyalty are overcoming racial and religious barriers to an increasing extent.

Though there is still a lack of desire on the part of some Malays to marry Chinese, and vice versa, in the cities and towns the general tendency is toward intermarriage. Among the Muslims, whether Malay or Indian, marriage outside the faith is frowned upon. A Muslim who marries a non-Muslim without permission is automatically excommunicated, and renounces the friendship of all Muslims. Thus, Malayan Muslims intermarry with Indians provided the latter are Muslims.

In the remote settlements of the central Malayan Peninsula and inland Borneo there is little contact between the different peoples. This is because of the lack of communications rather than feelings of enmity between particular groups. When the Muruts and Dyaks of Sarawak come into the towns or near-by plantations to work, they adapt themselves and become an integral part of a freely mixing society.

THE WAY OF THE CHINESE

The Chinese have had a great influence on the overall fabric of life in many South-east Asian countries. A hardworking and thrifty people, their contribution to the development of the region has been especially valuable in agriculture as well as in trade.

Although many Chinese whose families have been in Malaysia and Singapore for generations can no longer speak Chinese, having mixed with the Malays over a long period, some Chinese dialects still persist. Different waves of migration led to settling of different groups in different parts: the Teochews are concentrated in Kedah and Penang; the Hokkiens, shopkeepers and traders, live mainly in Singapore, Penang and Malacca, and the Hakkas are miners and farmers in northern Borneo.

Some customs and beliefs: The religions of the Chinese are Folk Religion, Confucianism, Taoism, Buddhism and Christianity. In Malaysia, Singapore and Brunei these religions have become modified, and to a certain extent, blended together. Religious festivals and processions and colourful temple ritual are an essential part of Chinese life, and much of the fascination of Singapore, or Kuala Lumpur, would be lost in the absence of the many ancient Chinese traditions.

Ancestor worship, an aspect of Chinese religion, is practised by all classes. It is based on the belief that people on earth can communicate with souls of people not incarnate, and that these may be influenced by events that take place on earth. A Chinese, knowing that he will have a say in matters concerning the family after his death, will try to avoid an accidental or violent death, since he believes that a disfigured body is something to be shunned.

According to an ancient Chinese belief the universe is governed by two forces, one negative and weak, called the *Yin*, and one positive and strong, called the *Yang*. Regions where these two forces meet in good accord are favourable ones for human settlement. When a person dies his body lies in harmony if buried in such a place, and

*A parking policewoman of Singapore.
Singapore is a mixture of the mystic orient
and the 20th century, the old and the new*

*With hundreds of miles of first-class roads in
Singapore, the trishaw is still a popular means
of transport, especially with the school children*

The Singapore housing and development plan allows for demolition of old houses and buildings and erection of modern high-rise apartments and office blocks

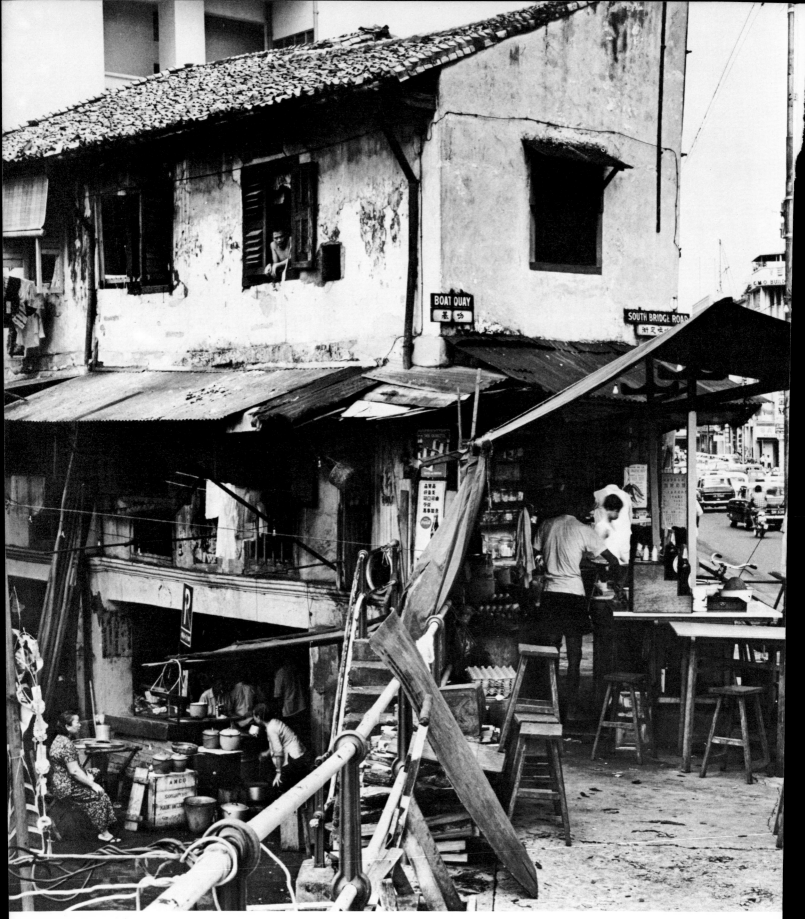

*Cross the Singapore River to the South Bridge
Road and you are in Chinatown. This building
has a waterfront cafe below, a sidewalk cafe
on South Bridge Road, a leathergoods shop,
and accommodation upstairs*

Singapore's Chinatown is one of the most colourful to be found anywhere. In small streets with names such as Nankin, Sago, Chin Chew, thousands of people mingle among the stalls of merchandise

An expanse of sail and a shallow draught allow these ships to call at isolated ports of South-east Asia to load their cargo for discharge in Singapore

The medium of Soon Thiam Keng Temple of the Monkey God in Singapore. The monkey is held sacred by the Buddhists because of the help given to the Chinese monk Hsuan Tsuang years ago on his pilgrimage to India from China

Singapore's foresight in housing has been so successful that it has won international acclaim and has been singled out as a model for developing countries

75% of the multi-racial population of Singapore are Chinese

Approximately 43% of the population of Singapore are under the age of 15. These Malay girls are part of the 15% that make up the Malay section

The babble of a hundred languages, the shrill cries of the street vendors, the chatter of conversation and the laughter of children make up the everyday scene in Singapore, where 200,000 travellers call each year

In a quiet niche, where space on this island of 224 square miles is at a premium, the lonely saw doctor works, oblivious to the noise and bustle of Singapore

Singapore time is 3 hours earlier than Sydney, 7 hours later than London, 9 hours and one day earlier than San Francisco. Working out international time is easy. Every degree of longitude is 4 minutes of time: if you travel west you subtract, and if you travel east you add on

*Victoria Memorial Hall in Empress Place in
Singapore was opened in 1862. Exhibitions
and cultural promotions are held here regu-
larly. Empress Place was named in memory of
Queen Victoria*

*There are many stately buildings in Johore;
from some of them you can see over Singapore
Island. Johore is 16 miles from Singapore, and
is on the northern end of the causeway over
the Straits of Johore*

*The majority of Indians in Singapore came
originally from southern India*

the soul can then use its influence in helping the family still on earth. A disturbance to a grave would put the soul out of accord with those on earth.

The front room of a Chinese house contains a small altar on which are placed ancestral tablets and photographs or paintings of ancestors. The names and dates of birth and death are written in gold on these wooden tablets. The family makes offerings at the altar, and at a certain time of the year, called the Feast of Ch'ing Meng, food, wine and money are placed at ancestors' graves.

Offerings are accompanied by the burning of joss sticks. Joss sticks are also used in the temple to find the answer to a problem. About 50 numbered sticks are shaken up and down in a container until one falls out on the floor. A printed paper on which are written, in verse form, answers for all the numbered sticks, is then referred to for the solution to the problem.

Astrology plays an important part in daily life. Chinese women consult their almanac to see if the day is propitious for certain chores. Astrologers declare which days of the week are lucky (good joss) and which are unlucky (bad joss). Many Chinese still use the lunar calendar, which divides the year into twelve lunar months, and the months into four weeks, full moon occurring on the 15th of each month. The western calendar serves for business purposes.

Marriages are performed according to the almanac, and if the day is right it is not unusual to see dozens of weddings taking place at once. Friends and relatives give money, rather than presents, to ensure that the wedding and the feast afterwards will be lavish. Once the bride is married, life becomes a battle with her mother-in-law, for Chinese mothers dote on their sons.

The Chinese are great believers in luck. The soothsayer and fortune-teller have been active since at least 1,800 B.C. Sneezing between certain hours of the day can bring good or bad luck. The flickering of an eyelid, moles or lines on the face, ringing sounds in the ears and dreams all have their particular significance and control good or bad joss. So do charms, talismans and mirrors. A mirror over a door in a Chinese house protects the family, for in reflecting light (the strong, *Yang* element) it keeps away evil spirits (the weaker, *Yin* element).

The Chinese is always mindful of his social and moral prestige in the community. To gain prestige or improve one's status by dubious or obvious means is to "lose face". The idea of using an agent or go-between in business deals or other undertakings ensures that if anything goes wrong the originator need not lose face. To save face is to compensate in some way for having lost face—an unsuccessful venture may be compensated for by making a large donation of money to a worthwhile cause.

THE MALAYS

The Malays form the largest racial group of the region and have, like the Chinese, a very high rate of natural increase. They constitute 80% of the indigenous population of Malaysia, 90% of which lives on the Malayan peninsula.

They are a people of diverse origins. Many came from Java and Sumatra, centuries ago. Even today, east coast Malays may feel themselves different from west coast Malays, but all feel a solidarity in being Malaysians, and are bound together by a common culture, the Muslim religion and Malaysian citizenship.

The Malay is generally short in stature, with a well-proportioned figure. His hair is black and straight and his complexion ranges from olive to dark brown. He has a wide, good-humoured smile, a prominent jaw and strong teeth. Loyal yet temperamental, he is quick to take offence, for he is proud and dignified, and his good manners are a legend. It has often been said that the Malay is not fond of work, but in fact, he will work long hours, from dawn till after dark even though he might prefer to sit and watch a cock-fight.

Until recently, the Malays have not had much opportunity to obtain a good education or develop their skills in many fields. For generations, British, Chinese and Indians dominated their region politically and commercially, and the Malays were restricted to practising certain occupations: they were clerks, chauffeurs or taxi drivers, farmers, fishermen, and policemen. Today they are still mainly farmers and fishermen, but an increasing number are moving into trading, professional and administrative positions.

Nearly all Malays are Muslims and participate in the ritual and ceremonies of their religion. Marriage is very elaborate: the religious ceremony itself, conducted by a *Kadhi*, is attended by the bridegroom and his witnesses but not by the bride. Afterwards, the groom walks in procession to the bride's house. At the entrance he is delayed by the female relatives of the bride, who demand a "tax" from him before permitting him to enter. The bridegroom then takes his place beside the bride for the enthronement ceremony (*Bersanding*). A few days later, the *Bersanding* ceremony is repeated at the house of the bridegroom's parents.

According to his religion, a Malay man can have up to four wives at one time, but Malay women demand that discarded wives be provided for. Such demands are largely respected, for Malayan women enjoy far greater freedom than Muslim women of other countries. There is no purdah, and many women and girls work in offices, shops and factories.

THE INDIANS AND PAKISTANIS

The Indians are not newcomers to Malaysia or to other places in South-east Asia. Long before the birth of Christ Indian traders sailed back and forth from India to the South-east Asian region. From the first century A.D. the islands of Indonesia, Malaysia, Formosa and the Philippines lay on the routes of trade between China, India, Arabia and the Mediterranean. Indian colonists spread to all these lands and at one time the region was referred to as Greater India.

There were several waves of migration, and Indians, Pakistanis and Ceylonese brought with them Hindu, Muslim and Hinayana Buddhist beliefs as well as strict social customs.

The caste system, with its people ranging from Brahmins to untouchables, is basic to Hindu society, and adds to the diversity of social structures within Malaysian communities. The importance of the family is upheld by custom and tradition; in Malaysia as in India, Indian women devote their whole efforts to the service of family and home. Marriages are often arranged to protect the interests of family and caste, and widows are forbidden to remarry.

The occupations of Indians and Pakistanis are usually inherited: they are shopkeepers, traders, money-lenders, clerks, taxi drivers, manual workers (especially rubber-tappers), policemen and politicians, and some are active in the professions.

History of the region

The Malayan peninsula and northern Borneo have had a colourful history. In earlier times Malaya and Singapore were ruled by the sultans of Malacca and Johore, and Sabah and Sarawak were part of the Sultanate of Brunei. In the whole region, the Chinese, Indians, Portuguese, Dutch, British, and to a lesser degree the French and Spaniards have played a part.

EARLY MIGRATIONS

It is believed that as early as 50,000 B.C. primitive men inhabited parts of the region, gaining a livelihood by hunting, agriculture and fishing. These people used stone implements. About 4,000 years ago, others came from south-western China. These were the Indonesians, who brought with them bronze tools. Some believe these people have always been in Indonesia and that the bronze tools were brought into the country as traded goods. The bronze age stemmed from the Tongking region many centuries before the Muslim era. The influence of the Chinese spread southward into Vietnam, where they established themselves and mixed with the people already living there. Out of this developed the Dongsong culture known for its bronze bells, drums and other items that portray a definite Chinese and Vietnamese mixture in their decoration. The Dongsong influence is found all over Malaysia, Indonesia, Borneo and the Philippines.

The next significant episode in the history of the Malayan peninsula was the movement of peoples from south-west China into the Red River delta. Later the Khmer people from Tibet came to the Mekong and the Mons started to spread into Lower Burma.

Advanced civilizations existed in the region at the beginning of the Christian era. Two thousand years ago Chinese traders from the north and Indian traders from Gujerat, the Bay of Bengal and southern India came into the Malayan region by sea. At that time there were trade routes to South-east Asia overland by way of Burma. Sea routes linked India, Arabia, and Africa; land routes linked these countries to Greece, Italy and other parts of Europe. The Romans took over both the sea and the overland routes. It has been recorded that the Romans travelled over the northern route to China in 97 A.D.

The Chinese were sailing to Borneo, Java and Sumatra as early as 206 B.C., but what really opened up the sea routes to South-east Asia was the discovery by Hippalus in 45 A.D. of the monsoon winds in the Indian Ocean. These made the journeys from India to South-east Asia and back very easy; they also aided the Chinese traders. During the months of April to September the winds blew from the south-west, and in the months of October to March they blew from the north-east. So the navigators sailed one way in one season and the other in the next.

With the coming of the Indians the people of Malaya and adjoining regions absorbed many Hindu ideas, and adopted the Indian practice of forming large kingdoms.

During the period when the Khmer people were building a great empire in Cambodia, to the south on the islands of the Indonesian Archipelago other kingdoms grew up. Wars were waged and the victors extended their realms until the empires of Sri Vijaya in Sumatra and Mataram in Java became all-powerful. Sri Vijaya took in all the country from the Sunda Straits and Sumatra, and the mainland as far as Cambodia.

Sri Vijaya traded with China, Bengal and the Coromandel coast of India in spices, sandalwood and other commodities. By this time Tanjore, on the east coast of India, and the Chola Kingdom to the south with its port at Pondicherry, had developed into a large trading empire. They had entered into trade with South-east Asia.

The control of the Malacca and Sunda Straits being in the hands of the Sri Vijaya meant that they could levy any amount of tax on vessels passing through. The Chola traders resented the high taxes and as a consequence waged war on Sri Vijaya. In 1025 the Chola sent a fleet and captured all the ports including Tumasik (later known as Singapore), and Ligor and Kedah in Malaya, and also the east coast ports of Sumatra. But the Chola could not maintain its hold on these places and Sri Vijaya soon took over once again. It was not until the latter part of the 14th century that Sri Vijaya was finally overthrown by the Majapahit empire from eastern Java, which became the dominating power in Indonesia, the Malayan peninsula, the south and west coasts of Borneo, the southern Celebes, and the Moluccas.

THE RISE OF MALACCA

By the 15th century the power of the Majapahit empire had also declined. This was brought about by the spread of Islam and the power of the empire in Malacca, which had grown into the biggest port in the area. Ships came in on one monsoon, unloaded their goods and reloaded them at the beginning of the next monsoon season. Malacca had control of the trading activities from east to west; it was the clearing house for the whole region—a prize for any kingdom in search of new conquests.

In an attempt to restore Chinese influence in South-east Asia, Parameswara, a prince from Palembang in Sumatra, sent envoys to China. He assisted Chinese traders and became recognized as the King of Malacca by the Chinese. Eventually, China regarded Malacca as one of its States.

But the Thai were also interested in gaining control of Malacca. By 1430 the Chinese were no longer able to maintain their interest there. The founder of the Ming Dynasty, Chu Yuan-chang, was more concerned with the consolidation of his people on the mainland than with places farther afield. Mongolian and Japanese invasions could not be resisted, and the Ming Dynasty came to an end in 1644.

The Thai demanded that Malacca pay tribute, which she refused to do. War broke out, and Malacca, even without the support of China, managed to repel the Thai and defeat the attack. From this period onward Malacca's power grew—till it exceeded that of the Majapahit empire. Sumatra and most of Malaya came under her control, Islam spread right throughout the Indonesian Archipelago and gradually up into Mindanao in the Philippines.

THE COMING OF THE EUROPEANS

The exploitation and colonization that followed the European conquests brought revolutionary changes to South-east Asia—especially in the spheres of religion, trade and government. It was the spices, described by Marco Polo in the 13th century, that first lured the Europeans to this part of the world.

40

The Portuguese: Equipped with the fastest ships afloat, the Portuguese were the first of the Europeans to occupy the region. They gained control of the Indian Ocean, captured Goa and then Malacca, under d'Albuquerque, Portuguese Governor of India. By the end of the 16th century they had built up an empire in South-east Asia.

St Francis Xavier was brought from India for the purpose of converting as many as possible to Christianity. Many Portuguese were not adverse to using force in converting the people, and skirmishes with the Muslims continued till the Dutch arrived.

The Dutch and English: Malacca fell to the Dutch in 1641. From then on the Portuguese empire dwindled until all that remained were Macau and Timor Flores.

The English East India Company had bases in the Spice Islands—visited by such seamen as Sir Francis Drake and Captain Kidd. But the Dutch ousted the English from the Archipelago, as well as the French, who had made half-hearted attempts to establish a French East India Company.

In 1795, at the time of the Napoleonic Wars, the British took over Malacca to prevent it from falling into French hands. In 1818 it was handed back to the Dutch, but became British again under the Anglo-Dutch Treaty of 1824.

THE RISE OF PENANG

In 1771 the English were looking for a place on the South-east Asian mainland, for their ships needed a port for repairs between India and China during the north-east monsoon season, and at the time of the Anglo-French wars it was imperative to have a base that could be used for naval ships as well as traders. France had the Island of Mauritius and could reach the Bay of Bengal faster than the British could get round the south of India from the west coast to the east.

Francis Light, a trader and ex-captain, took over the island of Penang in 1786 and established George Town, named after George III of England, and changed the name of the island to Prince of Wales Island. Some of the streets he named still exist today. In 1788 when the First Fleet arrived in Sydney Harbour there were already 200 houses in Penang.

Most of the people lived round the harbour foreshores and near the mangrove swamps—breeding grounds for dengue and malaria. In 1794 malaria caused the death of Francis Light. (His son William later became the planner of Adelaide in South Australia.)

By the early 1800s Penang had become acceptable to the British as a naval base, but not as a trade centre. Britain by then had grown in strength and feared no one. Her next move was to establish herself on the Malayan mainland.

RAFFLES IN SINGAPORE

Sir Stamford Raffles, having progressed from clerk to Governor of Fort Marlborough and Lieutenant Governor of Bencoolen and its dependencies, suggested the Island of Singapore as a potential free trade centre. He landed in 1819 on this almost uninhabited Island.

Singapore was then under the administration of the Sultan of Johore, appointed by the Bugis, a warrior race from the Celebes. Actually, the Island was ruled by the hereditary chief of Singapore, the Temenggong. On his arrival Raffles appointed Tengku Hussein Sultan of Johore, and a treaty was signed whereby the new Sultan was to receive 5,000 Spanish dollars a year and the Temenggong 3,000 dollars a year in return for rights granted the English East India Company to establish themselves in Singapore.

This treaty caused an uproar that resounded from Sumatra to London. The

East India Company itself was annoyed at having to protect yet another far-flung outpost that would not pay for its keep. The Dutch complained because they had regarded themselves patron and overseer of Johore. The officials in Penang believed the move would upset their position in island trade.

In 1824 the whole of the Island of Singapore was ceded to Britain for a lump sum and an increased pension to the Sultan and the Temenggong.

By 1839 the population was 10,000, being composed mostly of Chinese who had come down from the provinces of China. Trade was flourishing and Singapore was paying its way.

Under the Anglo-Dutch Treaty of London in 1824 the Dutch gave up all their territory on the mainland of Malaya, and the British gave up all theirs in the East Indies. Both nations guaranteed not to interfere in any way with each other's domain. This gave the British the power to progress in Malaya without any restriction from the Dutch. The Dutch had the same opportunity in the East Indies.

By 1832 the seat of British administration was transferred from Penang to Singapore, which was now a thriving and prosperous town. Raffles had made it a free port and so it became a trade centre. Goods from Europe arrived for transhipment and goods from China and the surrounding countries of South-east Asia were transhipped to Europe.

In 1833 the East India Company lost their monopoly of trading activities. Trade with China could now be undertaken by all British subjects. Then in 1858 the East India Company was dissolved and its authority taken over by the British Crown.

By 1860 Singapore had become the premier port, Penang the second, and Malacca third. Singapore had just over 80,000 people; of these, 50,000 were Chinese. Together, Singapore, Penang and Malacca had a total population of 272,000, of which 96,000 were Chinese.

In 1867 the Straits Settlements of Penang, Province Wellesley, Malacca and Singapore were taken over by the Colonial Office in London. The peninsula suffered years of widespread confusion: there were intrigues and wars between sultanates, and chiefs of villages levied taxes on river boats, or waged war on other chiefs to gain more power.

In 1874 the Governor of the Straits Settlements, Sir Andrew Clarke, arranged with the rulers for the appointment of British Advisers to Perak, Selangor and Sungei Ujong. But it took until 1891 for the system to become acceptable, and one Resident was murdered in the course of hostilities. (Johore did not request a British Adviser till 1914.)

In 1896 the Federated Malay States of Selangor, Perak, Negri Sembilan and Pahang were formed. The four States of Kedah, Perlis, Kelantan and Trengganu had been linked with Thailand. In 1909 a treaty with Siam transferred the suzerainty of these northern States to the British. With Johore, they then became the British protected Unfederated States of Malaya.

Britain was concerned not only with Malaya—Burma was a thorn in her side. The French too, were active to the north, and across the South China Sea. The Spaniards were entrenched in the Philippines, and south and closer to Malaya lay the Island of Borneo, with the Sultan of Brunei on the northern side and the Dutch on the south.

NORTHERN BORNEO

Brunei was mentioned as early as the 6th century in Chinese annals, and pottery dating back to the Sung Dynasty has been discovered in Sarawak. Kublai Khan sent an expedition in 1292 to establish a Chinese colony in northern Borneo, about the same time as Marco Polo mentioned that there was a thriving trade by junks between

Brunei and China. In the 14th century Brunei owed allegiance to Malacca, and in the 15th century, the influence of Islam spread there.

Magellan's ships arrived in 1521. The historian, Pigafetta, who sailed with Magellan, found a powerful and populous State, and wrote of the pomp and splendour of the Brunei Court. In 1530 the Portuguese established a mission and trading centre there. At this time, when Sultan Bolkiah was sovereign over the whole of Borneo, the Sulu Islands and part of the Philippines, Brunei was at the height of its power.

Toward the end of the 16th century this power had begun to decline, and Brunei was fast becoming a resort for pirates. The Spanish invasion of 1580, the expansion of the Dutch East India Company and the coming of the White Rajahs were contributing factors. By the late 19th century much of Brunei had been ceded to Sarawak and Sabah. In 1842 part of Brunei became the independent State of Sarawak, ceded to the first White Rajah, James Brooke, by the Sultan, in exchange for quelling a rebellion. (As Rajah, Brooke was a vassal of the Sultan.) In the latter half of the 19th century more and more territory was granted to Sarawak, which in 1888 became a British Protectorate, and was for three generations governed by the Brooke family.

The land of Sabah (British North Borneo) was ruled by the Sultans of Brunei and Sulu, until late in the 19th century. Brunei claimed the east coast to a point past Sandakan, and Sulu held the southern part, including some of what is now Indonesian Borneo.

Neither sultan was averse to receiving money in exchange for territory granted. In 1865 Claude Lee Moses, an American Consul in Brunei, arranged with the Sultan of Brunei to grant him territory in Sabah. In return for complete authority, Moses paid annual sums of money to the Sultan. He later sold his interests to a man named Joseph Torrey, another American, who managed to persuade the Sultan to confer on him the title of Rajah of Ambong and Marudu. Then came Gustafus Overbeck, an Austrian baron, in 1875. He bought Torrey's Sabah holdings and formed a partnership with the Dent brothers, who were also traders in Hong Kong. Overbeck acquired more land from the Sultan of Brunei in exchange for an annuity and became Rajah of Gaya and Sandakan. He extended the holdings of the partnership still further with land granted by the Sultan of Sulu, and by 1878 Overbeck and the Dents had the right to administer the whole of northern Borneo.

Shortly afterwards Dent bought out Overbeck and with support from London tried to establish permanent residence as a trader. The Spanish Government in the Philippines were strongly against this, even to the extent of sending naval vessels to Sandakan and asking Dent to pull down the Union Jack. The Spaniards claimed that Sulu and therefore Sabah was a Spanish protectorate.

Dent then approached the British Government for a charter. The last chartered company, the East India Company, had been wound up in 1869. The British Government altered its policy and granted Dent the charter to operate the British North Borneo Company, in 1881, reserving the right to supervise the administration of the Company. Lengthy discussions with the Spanish ensued, culminating in 1885 with an agreement that Spain recognize Britain's claim to northern Borneo, and Britain recognize Spain's claim to the Sulu Archipelago.

Together with Sarawak, in 1888, Sabah and Brunei became British protectorates. It was not until after World War II that the British North Borneo Company and the last white rajah, Sir Charles Vyner Brooke, relinquished all claims to their territories and handed them over to the British Government. Sarawak and Sabah were British colonies from 1946 till 1963 when they became part of Malaysia.

WORLD WAR II

Japan struck in December 1941, and within five months had occupied South-east

43

Asia. The defeat of the British, French, Dutch and Americans had a profound effect on the people of South-east Asia, especially when Japan promised independence for the various nations. In Malaya and Singapore the Japanese were intolerant of the Chinese but fostered the goodwill of the Malays and Indians. They formed a national army among the Indians and allowed the Malays to continue their authority in religion and titles to property. The Japanese intended to incorporate Malaya with Indonesia.

At the end of the war things were not easy for Malaysia. From 1948 till 1960 the long war against communist terrorists ensued, and today there are still skirmishes. Terrorists roam the Thai border, as well as the borders of Sarawak, Brunei and Sabah.

THE FEDERATION OF MALAYSIA

The word Malaysia is not a new word. It has been used since the 19th century to denote all the islands from Sumatra across to the Sulu Archipelago, and the Malayan peninsula. The people in the region were similar, and mostly Muslims; the common language was Malay.

The name Malaysia fell out of use at the beginning of the 20th century, when the two nations in power throughout the region were Britain and Holland. During this period the islands were known as Netherlands East Indies. Borneo was made up of Netherlands Borneo, and in the north, Rajah Brooke's little empire of Sarawak. On the mainland were the Federated States of Malaya, the Straits Settlements governed by the British High Commissioner, and the British Protectorate of the Unfederated States.

Since World War II significant changes have taken place. The Netherlands East Indies have become Indonesia, and British North Borneo is now Sabah. Sarawak and Sabah together form East Malaysia. Malaya has become West Malaysia and Singapore is an independent republic.

The Federation of Malaysia was created on September 16th, 1963. For the first time, colonies that had previously been administered as separate entities by Britain, merged to become one. These colonies—Malaya, Singapore, Sarawak and British North Borneo—became the Federation of Malaysia with Kuala Lumpur as the capital. Then in 1965 Singapore separated from Malaysia.

44

COLOUR

Chinese Buddhist priests in a temple in Malacca

Offerings to departed ancestors. It has been said that many a Catholic church has had its candles burnt in honour of a Chinese father or grandfather

The calligrapher spends most of his life writing letters or making charms for his Chinese clientele

A Chinese medium at the Monkey God Temple in Singapore. The medium gets ready for a consultation with devotees

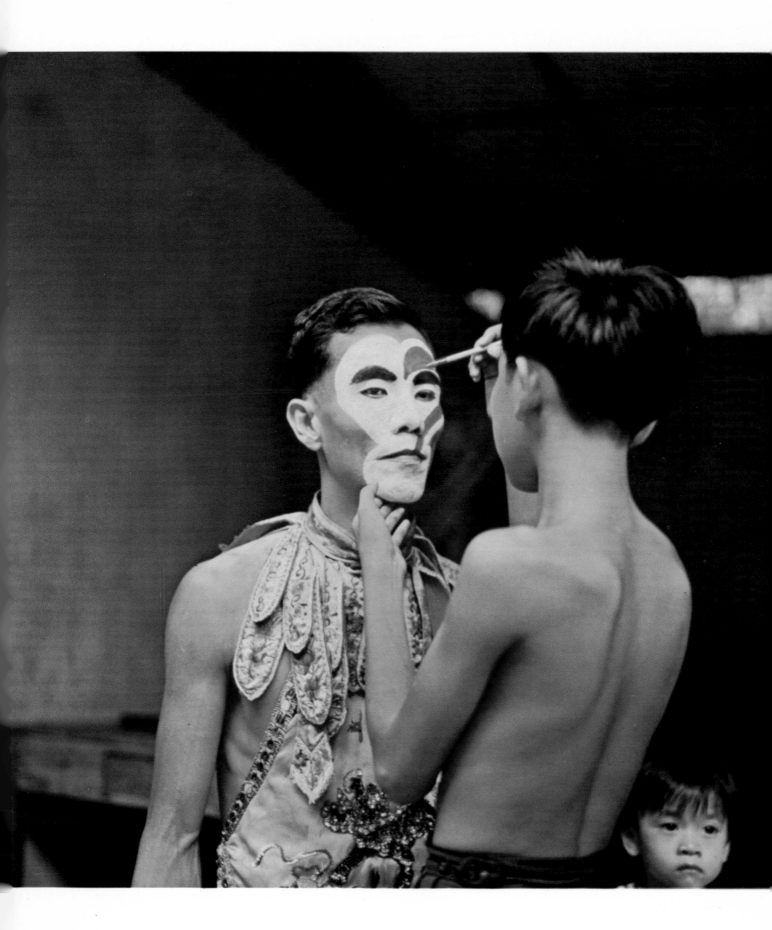

The Philippines were opposed to British North Borneo's becoming part of Malaysia—the Government there believed that British North Borneo was actually part of the Philippines, for in the 19th century the Sultan of Sulu had claimed the north and east portions of Borneo as his territory.

Having won West New Guinea from the Dutch, Indonesia's President Soekarno hoped to gain control of the whole archipelago. The day the Federation of Malaysia was proclaimed, Indonesian mobs sacked the British embassy in Djakarta, and the Government of Indonesia refused to recognize Malaysia. The Federation broke off diplomatic relations with Indonesia and the Philippines. Indonesia ceased trade with Malaysia, causing loss of revenue to Singapore and a great deal of unemployment. There were raids on Sabah and Sarawak by guerillas, and from August 1964 Indonesia made several attempts to land in West Malaysia.

The problem was taken to the United Nations, where the actions of Indonesia were deplored. In September, 1964, Soekarno agreed to a suggestion that Ayub Khan act as mediator, and in January, 1965, Indonesia withdrew from the United Nations. Soekarno's confrontation had not been successful from a military standpoint, but it did lead to racial and political unrest in Malaysia and a great loss of revenue. It has been largely the work of Soekarno's successor, President Suharto, to undo the damage done.

Brunei is not included in the Federation of Malaysia. It remains a separate Sultanate and a British Protectorate. An exceptionally wealthy country, Brunei has no inclination to become part of Malaysia; and for its part Malaysia insists on the unity of the areas of its east and west regions.

Geography of the region

The landform: Malaysia, Singapore, Borneo, Sumatra and Java are elevations of a submerged continent called Sunderland. In the Cambrian period the land began to form and build up on the Malayan peninsula. Later, in the Cretaceous period, large deposits of tin were formed by hydrothermal processes in this region, and about 60 million years ago the process of folding and warping began, and the land itself took shape. In the middle of the ice age of the Pleistocene period, Sunderland was exposed. When the ice melted, the water level rose and Sunderland was submerged, and the coastline began to take shape.

It has been estimated that the coastal plains of East Malaysia and those of Borneo are still becoming wider at the rate of ten feet every 30 years. Yet on the other hand, it has been stated that the rate of accretion along the east coast of Sumatra is between 60 and 500 meters each year. If this process continues Sumatra and the Malayan peninsula will be joined within 1,000 years.

The Malayan peninsula has eight mountain ranges running parallel to the coast, and half the peninsula is more than 500 feet above sea level. The Nakawn Range in the north-west forms part of the boundary between Thailand and West Malaysia. The Kedah-Singgora runs from Singgora in Thailand to central Kedah on the west coast. Parts of this range form the boundary between South Kedah and Province Wellesley. The Bintang Range extends from southern Thailand and parts of it form the Cameron Highland tourist resort called the Dindings. The main range, the Keldang, runs from Thailand right down the peninsula to Negri Sembilan with peaks from 3,000 to over 7,000 feet in height, gradually diminishing southward to end near Malacca. Among other ranges are the Benom, the East Coast and the Tahan—at 7,186 feet, Gunong Tahan is the highest peak in West Malaysia.

Geologically, West Malaysia consists of granite and nonvolcanic igneous rocks, alluvium and stratified rocks. Limestone outcrops jut out from flat ground, and large limestone caves can be found, such as the Batu Caves just north of Kuala Lumpur, with their vast caverns surrounded by jungle-clad hills.

The only flat lands are those along the coast on each side of the mountain ranges, the most extensive being on the western side of the ranges. On the east coast the plains are neither as wide nor are they continuous. The west coast has mud flats and mangrove swamps, whereas the east coast has long sandy beaches. The Island of Sumatra shields the west coast from the Indian Ocean, but the east coast has no protection from the South China Sea, and consequently winds and strong currents prevent swamps from forming.

A network of tributaries flows down from the mountains of the Malayan peninsula into the rivers which follow a parallel course to the ranges, and then turn outwards to the sea. The Sungei Pahang and Kelantan flow into the South China Sea, and the Perak into the Straits of Malacca. At their sources and in their upper reaches the rivers are quick-flowing, often with dangerous rapids and gorges. Lower, on the plains, the water takes on a muddy colour from the silt.

The land of Sarawak can be divided into three geographical zones: a swampy, alluvial coastal plain, undulating foothills intersected by mountain ranges, and a mountainous region in the interior—where Mount Murud, 7,950 feet, is the highest peak. A line of mountains makes a natural border in the south—the Kapuas Hulu, Hose and Usun Apau ranges, frequently above 4,500 feet in height with some summits over 8,000 feet, separate Sarawak from Indonesian Borneo in an almost continuous chain.

The coastal strip of mangrove swamps continues into Brunei: here, peat accumulates to a depth of 20 feet.

North-east of Brunei Bay, into Sabah, the long coastal plains peter out and are found only in isolated areas. Coral reefs close to the shore, together with mangrove swamps and river deltas, form sandy bars which make approaches to the coast very difficult. In parts, the ranges of mountains and lower hills reach right down to the coast, while the swamps extend inland for anything up to six miles. The mountains, running mainly parallel to the coast, rise fairly sharply from foothills to a height of 6,000 or 7,000 feet.

The main range of Sabah is the Crocker, which forms a barrier to communication close to the west coast, extending from the Sarawak border to the highest peak in South-east Asia, Mount Kinabalu (13,455 feet). To the east rise the volcanic Tawau Highlands, the Labuk Range, the Sir James Brooke Range and the Kilas Hills. A coastal plain, where most of the rubber, rice and coconuts are grown, stretches between the Crocker Range and the sea. The Tenom Valley, farther inland, contains some of the best agricultural land on the west coast.

Sarawak is drained by innumerable rivers flowing down from the mountains, winding through the jungle and emptying their waters into the South China Sea. The most navigable are the Rejang and the Baram—many others begin as a series of dangerous rapids in the mountains and are navigable for only part of their length.

The longest river in Sabah is the Kinabatangan, which begins its 350-mile journey to the sea in the Witti Range. Only 200 miles of it are navigable. Like most Borneo rivers, the Kinabatangan flows out to sea as a delta, through a maze of mangrove and palm. Smaller rivers of Sabah are the Segama, Labuk, Tungud, Inanam, Kawang and Papar. The Padas and Putatan rivers are used for navigation in west Sabah.

The climate: Temperatures in Malaysia are fairly constant—round 77°F. minimum and 88°F. maximum. In the Cameron Highlands the temperature is usually about 63°F., but a maximum of 80°F. and a minimum of 36°F. have been recorded.

At the summit of Mount Kinabulu in Sabah, temperatures as low as 36°F. have been known, though in the lower regions of northern Borneo the daily range is 71°F.–88°F. In Singapore, too, the climate is hot and humid—here the average maximum is 87°F. and the minimum 75°F.

In the night temperatures fall and humidity rises: when the temperature is at its lowest, humidity is at its highest. As a guide to gauging temperatures on the Malayan peninsula, you can calculate a drop of 1°F. for every 300 feet rise in altitude.

Very little variation occurs in the hours of daylight throughout the year. Alor Star, near the Thailand border, has a variation of 37 minutes, and in Singapore there is only six minutes' difference between the longest and the shortest day.

Malaysia, Singapore and Brunei are equatorial countries with the highest and most regular rainfall in the world. West Malaysia receives between 70 inches and 120 inches a year. From April to September the warm south-westerly monsoon blows, and from October to March the north-easterly monsoon brings most of the rain. November and December are the wettest months.

The east coast of the peninsula receives the highest rainfall, since it lies open to the monsoons blowing across the South China Sea. Kota Bharu is one of the wettest places along this coast. The west side is sheltered from the north-east monsoon by the Trengganu Highlands and the main range, and from the south-west monsoon by the mountains of Sumatra. Consequently, the rainfall here is lower. Kuala Klawang, about 50 miles north-west of Malacca, lies in the driest region.

Borneo has two seasons, the "wet" (April to September) and the "very wet" (October to March). The coastal areas of Sabah receive up to 200 inches of rain; farther inland, the rainfall decreases to about 62 inches. Sarawak receives from 100 to 160 inches over the whole country.

The soils: The soils of this tropical region are generally not as fertile as those of temperate areas, though there are extremely fertile pockets. On the Malayan peninsula, the soils of the western lowlands support coconuts, rice, and rubber crops, and in the south-west grow pineapples, vegetables and oil palm. Much of the eastern side of the peninsula—the wettest part—is infertile.

In Borneo, the frequent and heavy rains cause erosion, and remove minerals from the soil, especially in the hilly interior. Alluvial soils occur on the deltas and plains of the coast and interior, and support wet padi. Fertile volcanic soils in parts of east Sabah are used for the cultivation of export crops—abaca and oil palm. Rubber, the main export crop, grows on many types of soils. In the rainforest, which covers most of the region, the natural fertilizer deposited from rotting wood and other plant matter is not very deep, and the soils here are not nearly so fertile as those of tropical volcanic regions.

When visitors see the prolific growth of a tropical jungle—the huge trees, thick shrubs, vines and the plentiful supply of water—they may assume that the soil here is very fertile. But this is not so.

Where there is clearing and the sun reaches the earth, the constant heat helps to destroy plant nutrients of the soil. Soil temperature must remain below 75°F. for vegetation to break down naturally. In rainforest, the shade of its almost complete canopy keeps the soil temperature below this maximum. The trees shed leaves and branches; sometimes, because the trees are surface rooters, whole trees fall down. These are immediately attacked by ants and other insects. The condensed water falling from the tops of the trees and the rain help to decompose the fallen matter, which is then attacked by micro-organisms that turn the remains into acids and gases from which plant nutrients are freed. These are absorbed immediately, and the supply and demand continue. The cycle cannot be broken unless more humus is added artificially to form a residue. Thus, the luxurious growth of rainforests is not brought about by soil fertility but by the falling plant matter, the action of micro-organisms and the absorption of the humus formed.

This cycle will continue only while the forest stands. Take an axe or a bulldozer and clear the forest and you will have infertility. The soil temperature rises because of exposure to the sun, and the micro-organisms cannot live.

The plants: For thousands of years the whole of Malaya and Borneo was covered with forests. Even today there is very little clearing except where settlers have established themselves along coastlines and rivers. 70% of West Malaysia, 80% of Sabah and 73% of Sarawak are still forest-covered. Trees grow to a height of 180 feet or more, with girths of up to twelve feet. Some rise to 100 feet without a branch, with roots that leave the trunk several feet above the ground. Mangrove forests are found in swampy regions.

Four layers of growth can be distinguished in rainforests. The bottom layer is made up of ferns and seedlings, with leaves specially shaped to drain off water; the second layer consists of shrubs and small palms, and the third layer of trees that grow to a height of 80 feet or more, branching at 50 feet. Trees that are valuable for timber and reach 200 feet in height, form the top layer. The branches of these start on a level with the tops of the smaller trees of the third strata.

About 300 different kinds of trees have been found in the region; among them are screwpines, casuarinas, tree ferns, swamp laurels, nipah palms, santirai, dipterocarps (including the belian or Borneo iron wood), rattan (used for cricket bat handles), papaya, rambutans, mangos, breadfruit and dagger trees, and the giant colocasia in Sabah. Most are evergreens, shedding their leaves and renewing them continuously. A few kinds shed their leaves at irregular intervals, but not because of any climatic change.

Fungi and mosses thrive on the rain-soaked trunks of the forest. In savannah regions, tussock grasses grow as high as five feet. Lalang, an imperata species of grass, takes over in poor soil cleared of timber.

Among the hundreds of flowering plants found in Borneo is the insectivorous pitcher plant. The prey falls into the liquid contained in the trumpet-shaped leaf and becomes trapped there, for downward-pointing bristles prevent its retreat. Some pitcher plants can carry a quart of water in their pitcher after rain. The plant has medicinal uses.

The ant plant grows on trees in the rainforest. It is not insectivorous, but provides a home for ants in the network of channels contained in the round base of its stem. When a predator attacks the plant it is driven off by stings from the ants.

The durian fruit comes from a large evergreen—one of the many flowering

53

trees of Borneo. The flowers, red, pink or white, measure from two to four inches in width, and open in the late afternoon. The fruit is covered with thorn-like studs. It ripens to a yellowish-green, and divides into five sections with red or brown seeds along the edges of each. Easily recognized by its strong smell—something like sour cheese and garlic—the ripe durian attracts all kinds of jungle inhabitants, from tigers and pigs to insects and spiders.

The animals: Over half the total species of mammals, birds and reptiles can be found in Malaysia. There are over 200 kinds of snakes, including some that spit and some that "fly", and more than 550 kinds of birds.

The mammals include the elephant, orang-utan, gibbon and other monkeys, the two-horned rhinoceros, buffalo, barking deer, mouse deer, honey bear, tapir, wild cat, bat and lemur. Borneo is the home of the tarsier.

Illegal shooting of the rhinoceros and orang-utan is a problem for the Government in East Malaysia. The mother orang-utan is killed, and the young are taken and sold to zoos. The orang-utan can be found only in Borneo and Sumatra, and unless stricter measures are taken, these animals face extinction. The rhinoceros is shot for the supposed aphrodisiac contained in the horn.

Among the reptiles are many kinds of snakes, geckoes and lizards. Boas, pythons, vipers (of which the krait is commonest) and cobras—including the dangerous black and king cobras—occur in large numbers. The tree-snakes include two unusual kinds, the flying snake and the two-headed snake. The flying snake, sometimes called the golden snake, has the ability to flatten its body and glide swiftly from limb to limb. Contrary to common belief, it is venomous, and has fangs at the back of the upper jaw. The two-headed snake uses its tail as a decoy, by waving it backwards and forwards so that it resembles the head, while the true head remains poised ready to strike when the enemy comes within range.

Of the 300 species of geckoes found, the largest is the tokay; it grows to a length of 14 inches. All geckoes have toe pads, enabling them to grip the smoothest surfaces. The Indian blood-sucker, found on the Malayan peninsula, can change colour—when disturbed its throat swells and becomes reddish.

The legless lizards, often confused with snakes, can live to an age of 30 years or more. The female bears about 20 young at a time. The monitors found in the region sometimes grow to eight feet in length. The Komodo of Indonesia is the largest in the world.

Birdlife includes pelicans, cormorants, gulls, herons, ibises, spoonbills, ducks, owls, partridges, quail, cockatoos, parrots, hornbills, and swiftlets which build their nests in the limestone caves of northern Borneo. High prices are still paid for these nests, used by the Chinese to make birds'-nest soup. Gatherers have to climb long poles to scrape the nests off the roofs of the caves.

The rainforests teem with life. Green ants' nests hang from branches; caterpillars, worms, snails, scorpions, centipedes and huge spiders creep and crawl in the thick undergrowth of the forest floor.

The archer fish, found along the edges of the streams and estuaries of Borneo, shoots jets of water at insects. The prey falls into the water and is eaten. Another strange fish is the Borneo sucker fish. It has a series of sacs under its belly. It cannot swim very well and controls its movements by means of the sucker, swimming only when the waters are very calm.

Products of the land: Malaysia today is one of the richest and most economically stable countries in South-east Asia, and the people here enjoy a much higher standard of living than in most countries of the region. More than one-third of the world's

54

tin and rubber comes from Malaysia. Iron ore, timber, palm oil, pineapples, hemp, coconut oil, tea and coffee are main products. Important agricultural research is carried out by agricultural and forestry departments. As a result, ten million acres of land are now available for agriculture, and the output is steadily increasing.

One particularly successful discovery has been made—a new variety of rice of excellent grain quality and better resistance to disease. Improved varieties were first introduced by the agricultural department in 1964 and 1965. In 1966 the "miracle rice" of the Philippines was released. The traditional planting distance for rice is 12″ x 12″, and the new IR 8 miracle rice requires a planting distance of 8″ x 8″.

Malaysian farmers found it difficult to change their habits; they also complained of backaches caused by bending low for long periods to harvest this particular rice, which has a shorter stalk than other varieties.

In 1968 another variety was introduced which was to boost rice production more than ever before—a hybrid selection from the cross between an Indonesian and a Malaysian variety, combining the best characteristics of each. This new rice suits the Malaysian farmer better: the stalk is longer, the grain is larger and the planting distance is the traditional 12″ x 12″. It is the best quality rice so far, yielding 4,500 lb. an acre, and is soon to be used in other countries.

Rice is second to rubber in acreage; it covers about a million acres. This will increase in 1971 with the introduction of the River Muda (Malay peninsula) Irrigation Scheme, which is expected to bring nearly half a million more acres under cultivation. The new rice will be sown on farms averaging five acres in size, and the scheme will provide water for a second crop each year. About 70 % of the 50,000 farmers involved in the scheme are tenant farmers.

In Malaysia four and a half million acres are planted with rubber. The four important areas are Johore, Selangor, Perak and Negri Sembilan on the western side of the main range of the Malayan peninsula.

Rubber was first discovered in the exploration days of South America by the Spaniards, when sailors found natives playing with a bouncing ball. La Condamine, a Frenchman, found that this substance came from a tree, and in 1763 sent some back to Europe. An Englishman named Preisly discovered that rubber would erase pencil marks. Later Charles Goodyear mixed sulphur with rubber, heated it and obtained a harder product—the first vulcanized rubber.

The rubber plant grown in Malaysia originally came from England. In 1876 a man named Henry Wickham was sent to Brazil to smuggle out rubber seeds, which were a prohibited export at the time. The seeds he obtained grew into trees in London's Kew Gardens. Seedlings were sent to Ceylon, later to Singapore, and from Singapore to Malaya.

In Malaysia there are two kinds of rubber plantations. The farmer or small holder with only a few acres usually tended by his family taps the trees himself but does not have the facilities available to the holder of an "estate"—a plantation of 100 or more acres.

The small holder runs his rubber through a single roller many times and then dries it by hanging it up in the sun, or placing it on the hot road. This rubber sheet still has to be smoked. Some small holders have their own smoke houses but more often than not they sell the unsmoked sheet to a Towkay or Chinese trader who cures the rubber he buys. He cannot afford to cull his trees, or graft them. As long as the trees are giving latex he is satisfied. The Government helps the small holder to replant with new trees.

Since the introduction of synthetics, rubber growing has become a very scientific business, for only the best trees with the highest yield are of any economic use. Grafting control, soil erosion, the use of insecticides, and fertilization are all important aspects in the production of good rubber. Work is done not only in the field but also in the large laboratories of the Rubber Research Institute of Malaysia.

The large estate holders are well aware of the benefits to be gained by replanting with higher-yield trees, but the small holder is more reluctant to change. So far, more than a million acres of rubber have been replanted. Unselected seedling trees yield as little as 300 to 400 lb. an acre a year, but special varieties will yield up to 2,500 lb. an acre a year. It has been estimated that the production of rubber will be over one and a half million tons by 1976.

The rubber tapper is a specialist in his field. Work begins before daylight, when he is given some 300 trees to tap, usually contained in an area of about three and a half acres. The tapper cuts the bark of the tree at a slant following the circumference of the tree. This is done to allow the latex to flow downwards into a cup or receptacle that is placed at the bottom of the cut. The tapper has finished this part of his work by about 9 a.m., and goes off to await the flow of latex. At about 11 a.m. he returns to the tapped trees carrying two buckets. One is placed in a central position and the other is used to collect the latex from the receptacles.

When all the latex has been collected it is taken to the factory for processing. Here, it is first diluted with water, then formic acid is added to coagulate the rubber. Into this aluminium plates are inserted about one and a half inches apart. Several hours later the latex has set into slabs between the aluminium sheets. The rubber is washed and passed through a number of rollers which make it thinner and thinner. It then goes into a press which produces ribbed markings. Smoke curing takes about four or five days, then the rubber is ready for grading.

The Government has introduced a system of grading governed by technical specifications. All rubber is now marketed under the Standard Malaysian Rubber Scheme.

Coconuts and oil palm are other main crops. Coconuts grow on about half a million acres and oil palm, which was introduced into West Malaysia from Africa, on about 350,000 acres. Malaysia is the largest exporter of palm oil in the world. The oil is extracted from the fruit and ranges in colour from orange to a dull red. It is used in the manufacture of soap and grease. The white, pleasantly-scented oil from the palm kernel is used to make margarine and finer soaps, and stock food is made from the pressed kernels.

There are other crops such as coffee, pineapples, and a small acreage of cocoa. Malaysia is the third largest exporter of canned pineapples.

An area still to be developed is the Central Highlands of West Malaysia, regarded as one of the most fertile regions of the peninsula, but because of the importance of rubber, it has not been exploited to the fullest capacity.

Plans are underway to plant about 45,000 acres of maize on the east coast of the Malayan peninsula. A variety has been brought from Indonesia with a very high yield—about 4,000 lb. an acre.

West Malaysia

The Malayan peninsula, or West Malaysia, lies between 1 degree 20 minutes north and 6 degrees 40 minutes north in latitude and 99 degrees 35 minutes east to 104 degrees 20 minutes east longitude. The peninsula is about 500 miles long and is linked to Asia by the Kra Isthmus, which is about 18 miles wide at its narrowest part. At the southern point of the peninsula lies the island of Singapore, separated by the Strait of Johore but linked to the mainland by a causeway carrying road, rail and pedestrian traffic as well as large water supply pipes. West Malaysia covers an area of 50,886 square miles. From the coastline up into the high mountain ranges that form a spine from north to south, West Malaysia is a green and tropical country.

Where the thick forests have been cleared, agriculture is the essential pursuit. Rubber, copra, cocoa, coffee are major crops. A Chinese established the first commercial rubber crop near Malacca in 1898. Oil palm was brought to Malaya in the 1850s but only for cultivation as an ornamental palm. It was not until 1917 that its commercial potential was realized. The Portuguese introduced the pineapple to Malaya and a Chinese began canning this fruit in 1890. Today canned pineapple is a major export. Pepper, ginger, nutmeg, chillies, turmeric and many fruits and vegetables are secondary crops.

West Malaysians are becoming less dependent on imports as the years go by, and are buying more locally-produced goods. In recent years the Government has placed greater emphasis on industrialization to diversify the economy, and some form of secondary industry exists in most of the eleven states. Apart from the processing of agricultural products, growing industries include light engineering, car assembly, the manufacture of steel pipes, aluminium-ware, plastics and paints. Textile weaving is a cottage industry.

The Chinese held a monopoly of tin mining in Malaya until the end of the 19th century. Today, the tin fields of West Malaysia form part of the richest and largest tin-producing area in the world, that stretches from Burma to Thailand to East Malaysia and parts of Indonesia.

The Malayan peninsula has one of the finest networks of roads in South-east Asia. Regular rail services run between the main ports and inland cities, south to Singapore and north to Bangkok.

MALACCA

I left Singapore early one morning by Malaysia-Singapore Airlines and after a very short flight arrived in Malacca—a city where leisurely days can be spent exploring old buildings and learning of their colourful past.

Malacca was responsible for the establishment of trade between China, India, Arabia and Europe. It was from Malacca, too, that the influence of Islam spread to other parts of the Malayan peninsula. Founded in 1402 by Parameswara, who later became known as Megat Iskander Shah, the city remained subject to Chinese influence until it was captured by the Portuguese under d'Albuquerque in 1511. The Dutch took it in 1641, and in 1795 the British moved in to prevent it falling into French hands at the time of the Napoleonic wars.

Today, the old town contains relics of all these early influences—Chinese, Portuguese, Dutch and British. The Chang Hoon Teng is the oldest Chinese temple in Malaysia. Its ceremonial masts tower above Temple Street: outside, flowers and animals of porcelain and glass decorate its eaves; inside, beautifully carved lanterns painted in gold leaf, porcelain plaques, wood carvings and ancestor tablets adorn the walls. I was fortunate enough to see three yellow-robed priests conducting a service at the temple; their chanting, to the beating of gongs, brought to my mind stories of the mysterious rituals and ceremonies of ancient China.

Behind the Poh San Teng, another Chinese Temple, is a hill of historic significance, called Bukit China. In the 15th century the Sultan of Malacca's ambassador to the court of Peking arrived in Malacca with a gift in the form of the Ming Emperor's daughter, Princess Hong Lin Po, and her 500 attendants. The Princess was to marry the Sultan Mansur Shah. The Bukit China was set aside by the Sultan to accommodate the Princess and her 500 attendants. It became a burial ground in the mid-16th century, controlled by the Temple of Cheng Hoon Teng, and today it forms part of one of the largest cemeteries in Malaysia. Many of its graves are as old as the Ming dynasty.

The ruins of St Paul's church, built by the Portuguese in 1553, stand on the top of Residency Hill overlooking the city. For a short time this church held the body of St Francis Xavier, who worked as a missionary from India to the Moluccas. St Paul's has been a church for the Portuguese and the Dutch, as well as a fort and powder magazine for the British. The roof has now gone, but round the walls many old Dutch and Portuguese tombstones still stand, some dating back to the 16th century. A guide was there—a member of the Malacca Historical Society—to tell me the story of the church.

The Portuguese built the church of St Peter in 1710. This building is remarkable for its facade of eastern and occidental architecture. The gateway of Porta de Santiago still stands as the last relic of the old Portuguese fortress demolished by the British in 1807.

Dutch architecture in Malacca dates from the mid-17th century. Christ Church, built of reddish brick, has the louvre windows, heavy hardwood doors and beaming typical of early Dutch buildings. On the other side of the city circle stands the Stadthuys, an older and remarkably solid Dutch building, now used as Government offices.

The town circle itself becomes a gathering place for Malaccans: looking across from the Stadthuys I saw a man demonstrating the potency of a strange elixir, and judging by the size of the audience round him, his arguments were most effective. Behind him, over the tree-lined nature strips dividing the traffic, I could see the Tan Kim Seng Bridge over the Malacca River—an excellent vantage point from which to view the beamy river boats being piloted up the river to unload their cargoes.

Along each side of the river the houses stand flush with the water's edge, and from each house platforms have been built out over the river. The boats tie up at these platforms and there is a flurry of activity as dozens of men start to unload cargo. They carry everything on their shoulders along narrow planks placed between the small wharves and gunwales of the boats. Looking in the other direction back towards the sea I glimpsed other boats moving into the river to tie up at the large godown near the entrance of the town. Boats have been coming and going in this way for hundreds of years, long before Marco Polo's visit in 1292.

Just before the tropic night fell I walked about the city to see the shops and their wares. Malacca changes its personality with the coming of night—the place becomes a blaze of lights as people leave their work and fill the town at dusk. Some pedal in on bicycles, set up their mobile shops, turn on the lights and are ready for business. I was told of one Malaccan who has earnt a trip to Japan for his holiday by selling in the streets at night. Another, who has worked hard selling rice cakes, can send his children to England for higher education.

As I walked among the stalls I heard a voice ask "How have you enjoyed your stay in Malacca?" Turning round, I saw a smiling Chinese. I replied that I was most impressed with the place. After a short chat, my new friend, Doctor Wong, suggested that we go for a drive and later have dinner with his wife and friends. Meeting someone like this is the best way to learn about any country. That evening, we went to a restaurant in Newcome Road, where I was served a very tender and tasty steak—one of the largest I have ever tackled.

A Chinese house: I asked Dr Wong where I could go to see how the Chinese live. He replied, "But the Chinese are like everyone else." "Yes, I agree," I said, "but can I see through a Chinese house?" At that, he took me across the Tam Kim Sengs Bridge, turned into the first cross street and then into Heeren Street—a narrow street allowing just enough room for two cars to pass at a time. Some of the houses are built flush with the street; others have small porches. We pulled up and waited for an Indian-driven bullock cart, loaded with grass, to pass slowly by.

A large, three-storeyed house with a small tiled roof jutting over the entrance stood before us. The top floors were painted white, their rectangular windows framed by the wooden shutters so common in Malacca. The entrance porch was supported by two huge wooden pillars. Above the large double door which was intricately carved and painted in gold leaf, a plaque was set into the wall. This had been carved in stipple effect and painted in gold leaf as well, with Chinese characters in black enamel. On each side of the door, scenes depicting bamboo trees and jungle animals— all in gold leaf—decorated tall wooden screens. The floor of the porch, raised to a height of 18 inches above street level, was laid with marble slabs.

When first built, several hundred years ago, the houses jutted out over the water of the Malacca Straits, so that rubbish could be thrown out of the windows directly into the ocean. The foreshores have since been reclaimed, and these houses now stand on high ground well back from the water's edge.

The first room of the house we visited measured about 40 feet by 50 feet and contained hand-carved chairs and tables on a marble floor. Each chair was made of a black wood, its back inlaid with marble, its legs and sides encrusted with mother of pearl in flower or geometric motifs. In the centre of the room stood an altar with portraits of ancestors, and the air was filled with the smell of burning sandalwood.

The next room had glass-doored cupboards built into two of the walls. Behind the glass, dozens of crockery sets lined the shelves, ranging from the finest china to the heavy, utility kind. The crockery used is selected according to the status of the visitor.

My host ushered me through an elaborately carved doorway into another room where a semi-circular wall about three feet high partly enclosed a sunken bath and bath-house, both in glazed tile. This bath was over 300 years old. The roof of the room was open in places, and designed in such a way as to allow the sun to filter through without letting the rain in.

The furniture of the upstairs rooms was not so elaborate, since this part of the house is used for sleeping rather than entertaining. The floors here were of timber. The ground floor also contained a kitchen and a general purpose room, and it was from here that rubbish was tossed from the windows into the sea many years ago.

From Malacca to the capital, Kuala Lumpur, is about 90 miles by air. This fast-developing city holds the seat of the Malaysian Government and a population of some 500,000. It attracts thousands of visitors every year—among them industrialists, golf-players and car-racing enthusiasts. It is a city of contrasts: of old and new, and of many races, where striking contemporary architecture has found its place beside picturesque old buildings of Chinese and Persian influence, Indian temples and Malay kampongs. The visitor has the choice of buses, taxis and trishaws to take him over the sprawling metropolis.

A little over 100 years ago Kuala Lumpur was sited by a party of 87 men travelling up the Klang River in search of tin. When they came to the entrance of the Gombak River they walked inland and struck rich tin deposits. Kuala Lumpur began as Ampang, a tiny outpost for tin miners. Today Ampang is one of the city's suburbs.

Old sanscrit stories of Indian voyages to the East mention the tin mines of the Malayan peninsula as early as 300 B.C. The metal is still being taken here from the open cut mines, though the output today is much less than in past years. I visited mines not far from the site of the original finds. The miners, who work seven days a week, direct high-pressure hoses at the banks of the open cut to break down the tin-bearing gravel. This gravel is pumped up into sluice boxes for recovery of the tin ore. A few miles north of Kuala Lumpur, on the way to the Batu Caves (remarkable for their vast limestone caverns) you can see huge dredges. Dredging is the more practical method of obtaining tin from the soil—a chain of buckets scoops the tin-bearing gravel onto the sifting mechanism of the dredge.

On my way to see the tin mines I stopped to view the Istana, or palace of the Agong. While taking pictures I removed the magazine slide from my camera, and when I reached the tin mines I found that my slide was missing. We returned to the hotel about three hours later, and I still could not find the slide. Then I realized I had left it on the wall of the fence outside the Agong's palace, and drove back there. Hundreds of people had walked past the palace in the meantime, yet I found the bright aluminium shutter where I had left it. In Sabah, too, I admired the honesty of the Malaysians when I saw unlocked cars left with expensive equipment on the seats.

Although Malaysia is multi-racial, and most Malaysians speak many languages, this does not mean that everyone can read or understand all the different languages spoken. The Chinese come from many parts of China, the Indians from many parts of India, and as a result, a whole collection of dialects has survived. At my hotel I asked a Chinese girl to find an address for me in the telephone book. She was unable to read the address, which was written in Malay, and called an Indian over for help. He called a second Indian, and another Chinese also offered to be of help. The conversation proceeded in Tamil, Cantonese, and Malay, with interjections in English, but in the end, I got the address I was looking for.

A children's procession: On the morning of the Anniversary of Independence I went to the Stadium Merdeka in Kuala Lumpur to watch the procession and display of children.

I found crowds of children milling round outside. Proud parents, visitors and hundreds of diplomats had come along as well. I entered the stadium thinking that this was going to be just another children's rally such as can be seen at home or anywhere else.

I found a seat upstairs in the stand and looked out across the wide arena at the thousands of children with their many different uniforms forming bright and contrasting bands of colour. Before long a band marched into the arena, followed by the well-trained ranks of performers, in colourful and orderly procession. Each school was led by its own standard-bearers. When all the children had marched round the ring they formed groups and gave a display of callisthenics to music.

Then a group of several hundred girls, with violet chiffon scarves floating about them, performed a series of intricate exercises and a ballet set to European music. It must have taken them many hours of planning and rehearsal to attain such excellence.

The boys showed their skill at gymnastics, and played songs on the bamboo, an Indonesian instrument that emits notes when shaken—rather like those of an organ. The players, with instruments ranging from bass to treble, stood in a long line in front of the conductor. Their performance included excerpts from operetta, Malay music, and songs well known to the western world.

One event created much excitement among the younger onlookers. It was a mock battle, enacted by soldiers portraying the peril of the communist threat to Malaysia that took 22 years to defeat. The firing of rounds, with dummy hand-grenades, produced a very realistic effect.

Kite-flying: The Malays are kite fliers with centuries of tradition behind them. The art of Wau-kite flying has its origins in Malayan mythology, and has been handed down over hundreds of years. The *Wau Bulan*, known as the moon kite because its tail is shaped like the sickle moon, comes from the east coast. With a wing span of eight feet and a height of about ten feet, it is the largest kite to be flown in Malaysia.

Today, matches are held from time to time. The frames of the kites are made of bamboo covered with waterproof paper. In earlier times broad leaves were used to cover the frames—these were very skilfully sewn together so that the wind could not blow them apart. Some of the larger kites took up to three weeks to make, being more than five feet wide and of intricate design. Many have an attachment called a *busur* which is like a bow, and gives a humming sound when flying through the air. The *busur* is usually made of bamboo, and the string which vibrates and causes the humming noise is cut from the *daunmulon* leaf. On a moonlight night one can hear this humming sound high above when the kites are left in the air after dark in the kite-flying season. The noise is supposed to lull the owner to sleep; when a storm looms up the sound of the humming changes and the owner awakens and hauls his kite to safety.

Launching is a two-man job. The launcher, or *Juru Anjung*, holds the centre of the kite in one hand and string in the other. The second man stands a short distance away holding the roll of string, which can be anything from 600 feet to 1,800 feet long. Nowadays, plastic string is used, being stronger than any other. The *Juru Anjung* launches the kite by throwing it upward to the wind, while his off-sider plays out the string. The kites can reach an altitude of 1,500 feet but are usually flown at about 600 feet.

It is difficult to bring down a kite without damaging it. The launcher waits till the kite comes within reach and then quickly grabs it, while the second man tries to prevent it diving straight into the ground by carefully manipulating the string.

PENANG

From Kuala Lumpur to Penang is a short flight by Malaysia-Singapore Airlines. The Island of Penang covers an area of 110 square miles, just off the mainland of West Malaysia. It is considered one of the most pleasant islands in the tropical region of South-east Asia. Georgetown, the main city, with a population of nearly 240,000, has a history that goes back long before the British occupation in 1786. At that time Penang was called Prince of Wales Island.

I spent my first evening walking along the streets of Georgetown watching the trishaw drivers and the people in the streets. The atmosphere is leisurely and friendly. I watched an Indian food seller walk about calling out his wares. He carried the food in two cane baskets hanging from a long pole supported across his shoulders, Chinese fashion. Stopping near a row of trishaw drivers, he placed the two baskets on the ground and displayed his food. To do so, he had to take out separate containers, each with a different item. After the customer had made his selection, the food seller opened another small basket, produced bowls and eating utensils, and ladled out the food. He was paid, and when his customers had finished he placed everything back again, picked up the baskets and went on his way to other customers.

All the shops in Penang stay open till late in the evening, and when business is over for the night, the trishaw drivers curl up in their vehicles, pull a newspaper or a piece of canvas over themselves and go to sleep.

Taxis are plentiful on the island, but though drivers are bound by law to have meters installed, the first thing I noticed was that these are never used. The fares, however, are usually correct.

The visitor can drive right round the island, a distance of 46 miles, on a well-made tar road. A short distance from the city limits lies the village of Tanjong Bungah. This once very quiet village has been developed into a lively holiday resort with hotels, restaurants and clubs. Farther along the road, Mount Pleasure gives the traveller an excellent view of the mainland of West Malaysia, and to the north, the mountains near the border of Thailand. All along the route small and large inlets with sandy beaches break the coastline. The road passes through rubber plantations where you can watch the rubber tappers at work in the early morning or late afternoon. Along the valleys, cloves and nutmeg crops grow.

Sometimes, looking out to sea, the outline of a ship can be seen ploughing its way through the Malacca Straits, which separate Penang from Sumatra. Closer to shore fishermen who have caught their haul are busily packing away their gear ready for the next day's work.

Temples and shrines: Along the road I saw a white rock with joss sticks burning beside it. This was a Chinese shrine. Both the Confucians and the Hindus use rocks or trees as shrines where passers-by can stop and pray. The Hindus place lime on a metal trident, with a piece of red cloth tied round the bottom. Underneath the trident is a piece of charcoal impregnated with joss stick powder, which, when burnt, gives off smoke and a pleasant smell. The joss stick powder is made from the sandalwood tree. The sandalwood is crushed to a powder which is then bound with tapioca flour, rolled onto a bamboo stick and dried in the sun. For colouring, paint powder is mixed in. Most of the sandalwood comes to the factories from the east coast of West Malaysia. Joss sticks come in various sizes up to about four feet in length and one foot in diameter. The larger sticks are decorated with a coiled dragon, beautifully carved and coloured either white, yellow or red. They burn continuously for about 17 hours, and sell for $M45.

Temples abound in Penang. Inside one of the many I saw, the Chinese Snake Temple, green snakes twine themselves round small bushes. At night, hens' eggs are left beneath the bushes for the snakes to eat. I was greeted by an attendant saying "Come and see the snakes, sir". He picked one up, and I asked what kind it was. "Oh, these are the pit viper," he replied. They did not look like pit vipers at all, and on making enquiries later I was told they were harmless green tree snakes.

The Thai Temple is remarkable. At the far end reclines a huge statue of Buddha; along one wall, hundreds of small gold Buddhas stand out against a blue background; along another, similar gold Buddhas are set against a red background. The pillars

62

are painted with a vermilion lacquer, their frieze of leaves in gold leaf. In front of the reclining Buddha, in the light of a dozen red candles, the rotund priest sat cross-legged on a chair receiving and administering to his devotees. He seemed like a Buddha himself.

A dental hospital for children: Penang has a dental hospital with a difference. It is a large place, set up to treat as many children between the ages of four and twelve as possible, and every effort is made to create a different image of the dentist and remove all fear from the young patient's mind. When the child comes into the hospital he is given something to occupy him while waiting—he can play games or look at picture books. In the treatment room, he sits in a dental chair specially designed for the comfort of children.

Malaysian girls, trained as dental assistants, instruct the children in dental hygiene, insert fillings, and perform other routine duties so that the qualified dentist is free to concentrate on treatment of a major nature.

The Penang hospital has proved a successful venture, worth close study. In the hour or two I spent there, I did not hear a single child cry.

CONSTITUTION AND GOVERNMENT OF MALAYSIA

The seat of Government of Malaysia is Kuala Lumpur, in West Malaysia. The Supreme Head of Malaysia is called the Yang di-Pertuan Agong. He is commonly known as the King or Supreme Sovereign. His wife, the Raja Permaisuri Agong, is second in order of State precedence. The King is elected at the Conference of Rulers, by the nine State Rulers—the only people eligible for the throne. Voting is by secret ballot and the King remains in office for five years. A deputy, called the Timbalan, is elected in the same way.

On his election the King must relinquish all his powers as Ruler of his particular State for the period of his appointment to the Supreme Sovereign position. He appoints a regent to act on his behalf in his State. In the event of the King's death, the position is filled in the usual way by election.

Since he is regarded as the "fountain of justice" the King has the power to appoint a Prime Minister as well as High Court and Federal Judges. He is supreme commander of the armed forces and head of the Muslim religion in Malaysia. All acts of government pass through his hands, though as a constitutional monarch he is obliged to accept the advice of the Prime Minister.

The Malaysian Parliament has two houses: the Senate, or Dewan Negara, and the House of Representatives, or Dewan Raayat. The 60 members of the Senate are drawn from East and West Malaysia: 28 are elected, and 32 are appointed by the Yang di-Pertuan Agong. The Senate elects a President and Deputy President from among its members, and holds office for six years. The House of Representatives has 144 elected members—104 are from the eleven West Malaysian States, 24 from Sarawak and 16 from Sabah—and serves for a five-year period. All bills must be passed by both Houses of Parliament before being presented to the Yang di-Pertuan Agong for the Royal Assent in order to become law.

The King appoints a Cabinet consisting of the Prime Minister and an unspeci-fied number of ministers who must be active members of Parliament. The Cabinet meets about once a week under the chairmanship of the Prime Minister to formulate the policy of government.

The Public Services, both civilian and military, are non-political and owe loyalty not to the ruling party but to the King and the State Rulers.

Each of the eleven West Malaysian States as well as Sarawak and Sabah, has a State Ruler, in some cases called a Governor. Each of the 13 States has its own written constitution and Legislative Assembly. A speaker presides over each Legislative Assembly.

For administrative purposes, the States in West Malaysia are divided into districts, each under a District Officer, responsible for local matters. In Sabah the districts are grouped into four Residencies—West Coast, Interior, Sandakan and Tawau—each of which is administered by a Resident. Sarawak groups its districts into five provinces known as Divisions, each under a Resident.

64

S. B. Pannefort

East Malaysia

East Malaysia extends over an area of 76,458 square miles in the north-east and north-west of the island of Borneo. It is made up of two States, Sabah and Sarawak. The independent sultanate of Brunei, sandwiched in between, covers an area of 2,226 square miles.

The name Borneo for years has been suggestive of headhunters, dark jungle adventures, white rajahs, the North Borneo Company and the Sultan of Brunei. All have been subjects of fascinating stories set in a land remote from the rest of the world.

Today, with the development of oil resources and fast plane travel, the island of Borneo is no longer remote, but takes an active place in the commerce of nations.

Sarawak

LAND OF JUNGLES AND RIVERS

The land of Sarawak extends along the north-east coast of Borneo for 450 miles, varying in width from 40 to 120 miles. Its population totals nearly 900,000.

It is a tropical land with a complex network of rivers winding through jungle and cultivation to the South China Sea. The most navigable of these rivers are the Rejang, the Baram and the Sarawak. Much of the country is covered by tropical rainforest, and until recently was inaccessible, except by rivers—which are still the main thoroughfares throughout Borneo. Launches and long dug-out canoes with outboard motors make an endless "put-put" noise that is heard all over the island.

The economy of Sarawak centres round forestry, oil refining, gold mining and agriculture. Oil is imported from Brunei and exported as crude oil and refined products. Timber is floated down the rivers as rafts; and rubber, pepper, bauxite, rattan, charcoal, illipe nut, incense, copra, sago, and jelutong gum are loaded on small sea-going vessels at Kuching for export. Imports include textiles, foodstuffs, machinery, beverages, tobacco and manufactured goods.

Government schemes for increasing agricultural production are hindered only by inadequate communications. Plans have been made for draining large areas to improve padi crops, for training courses for farmers, and for extensions to the electricity and water supplies. More roads are being built to make this development possible.

The five divisions: For administration Sarawak falls into five divisions. Twenty-three district councils are distributed over the five divisions—all local authorities being elected by secret ballot.

Kuching, capital of Sarawak, is also the administrative centre of the First Division. Here you can visit the old Astana, the palace of the White Rajahs, built in 1870, the Sarawak Museum—renowned for its natural history and ethnological exhibits, or one of the several ornate Chinese temples. Kampongs (native villages) surround the city, and ten miles of mangrove swamps stretch to the coast, with many streams on their way through to form a delta.

Bau and environs, a few miles to the south-west, was a centre of gold-mining for over 1,000 years. The surface mines are now lakes suitable for swimming. Lake Tai Parit is 200 feet deep. The most westerly town, Lundu, lies beneath the mountain Gunong Gading, quite close to the Indonesian border. Here, Chinese and Malays make up most of the population, mixing with Land Dyaks and Ibans.

The Second Division was originally the main Iban stronghold of Sarawak, and Simanggang, the capital, lies on the banks of the Batang Lupar River. In 1849 the White Rajah, Sir James Brooke, established a fort farther upstream at the mouth of the Skrang River—a swift flowing tributary of the Batang Lupar.

Between the headwaters of the Saribas and Skrang rivers is a saddle-back mountain called Sadok. Here, the Dyak outlaw Rentap repelled two expeditions of the White Rajah in 1857 and 1859. At Betong, on the Saribas, the Government District Officer is housed in an old ironwood fort—still complete with drawbridge.

Saratok, another district in the Second Division, covers an area drained by the Krian and the Seblak rivers. It is a Sea Dyak region, though one of the largest Malay kampongs in Sarawak lies at the mouth of the Krian. Saratok is the centre of a pioneer venture in rural education known as the Saratok Community Development Scheme.

In 1850, Sir James Brooke was held responsible for the massacre of Iban pirates by a Royal Navy Unit near Kabong, round the sandbanks of the Beting Marau River. The British Government censured the White Rajah for this action, but it was later shown that the charges against Brooke were unfounded.

The Third Division has its headquarters at Sibu, about 60 miles from Kuching by outboard canoe. From this island town, at the confluence of the Rejang and the Igan rivers, boats travel upstream into the dense Borneo country—dark jungles, untouched by any marks of the present-day. The streams of the huge Rejang delta wind their way from Sibu to the coast. The population here consists of Chinese, Malays, Melanaus and Sea Dyaks.

Mukah, headquarters of the Coast District is in the centre of the sago-growing country. The population here is mainly Melanau, but a large Iban community inhabits the Oya, Mukah and Balingian river areas. Kanowit, some thirty miles up the Rejang from Sibu, was one of the first District headquarters established in the Third Division. In 1859 two of the Rajah's officers, Fox and Steele, were murdered here by the Kanowits, a group related to the Kayans and Melanaus.

Farther inland is Kapit, the headquarters of a district covering about 15,000 square miles drained by the Balleh, Balui, Upper Rejang, Belaga and Katibas rivers. At Kapit, the Rejang rises as much as 40 feet in a night when flood waters pour down. The banks become muddy cliffs in the dry season. Beyond Kapit, dangerous rapids make navigation difficult and hazardous. Inland to Nanga Pila and beyond live the Kayans, Kenyahs, Penans, Kejamins and Skapans. Elephants are used by Chinese timber millers for hauling timber in the Ba Valley, at Kapit.

The Fourth Division covers a narrow coastal strip between Bintulu and the Brunei border. The Baram, Bintulu and Miri districts here are drained by the Baram, Miri, Sibuti, Kemena and Tatua rivers.

70

Miri, capital of the Division and third largest town in Sarawak, attained significance in 1909 when oil was first discovered there. The oilfield is still in operation, though refining of oil from Brunei has become the main industry. Chinese, Malays, Dyaks and Kedayans live here.

The caves of the limestone hills at Miri contain the birds' nests used in the soup industry by the Chinese. Archaeological excavations here produced evidence of human habitation as far back as 50,000 years ago.

The district of Bintulu lies in the valleys of the Kemena and Tatau rivers. Here, the peak of Bukit Mersing rises to 3,344 feet in the volcanic Tau range.

Marudi is the main town of the Baram district. One of the tributaries of the Baram, the Akah, is reputed to be the most dangerous river in Sarawak, and the Kayans and Kenyahs of the Baram are probably the best boatmen in the country. In the highlands at the head of the Baram live the Kelabits. The wandering Penans inhabit the hills of the Baram and Bintulu districts and the upper reaches of the Rejang.

The Fifth Division lies on the far side of Brunei next to Sabah. This country became part of Sarawak in stages—the Trusan Valley in 1884, the Limbang in 1890, and the Lawas District in 1905. Malays, Kadazans, Bisayas, Kelabits, Dyaks and Muruts inhabit the area. The Limbang Valley is one of the best agricultural areas in Sarawak. Chinese farmers grew pepper here in the 18th century—and perhaps long before that. It once supported large communities of Muruts, and relics of early Indian travellers have been found. Today oil palms grow in the valley. Its upper reaches are mountainous, dominated by the double peaks of Batu Lawi.

The Trusan River is not navigable for much of its course. The Lawas River is entirely navigable, and river traffic is the only means of transport here. Much of the country is travelled on foot—Lawas is about seven days' walk from the Indonesian border.

PEOPLES OF SARAWAK

There are at least ten racial groups in Sarawak. Some are known as Sea Dyaks, because of their habit of going to sea as war parties, others are known as Land Dyaks.

The Ibans (these are Sea Dyaks) are the largest group. They came from Indonesia in the 18th and 19th centuries, and over the years have established themselves in many parts of Sarawak. An energetic and highly intelligent people, they are like the Malays in appearance. Old skulls hanging in little rattan baskets from joists in the longhouses are evidence of the earlier adventures of the Ibans—once headhunters and pirates.

The second largest group are the Bidayuhs (these are Land Dyaks), who live in longhouses and eke out an existence by planting dry padi. First they burn off the jungle, then make holes for the seeds by thrusting a long stick into the ground. Each area is cultivated for about two or three years before another area is burnt off and cleared. The original plot is then left fallow. The demands on the soil have increased with the growing population, bringing about a loss in soil fertility. The Bidayuhs are related to the Land Dyaks of Kalimantan, and grant their women full rights in community life.

Once the most formidable enemies of the Ibans were the Kayans and the Kenyahs, who came to Sarawak from the north-east and settled inland near the sources of the Rejang and Baram rivers. Large numbers of these tribes were wiped out by malaria, but since the disease has been brought under control they are again on the increase. They are taller and fairer than the Ibans, and particularly musical. The Kenyahs and Kayans have an aristocratic governing system, whereas the Ibans elect their chiefs.

71

The Kayans are well known for their wood carvings and paintings. The same painting of a human eye can be seen on the boats and houses of the Kayans as is found in Timor and Singapore. The women are expert weavers, their woven designs often delicately incrusted with beads. Shells, too, are used by the Kayans in decorative crafts. Years before the coming of the Europeans, shells (as well as beads, gongs and other objects) were used as money in Borneo, as they were in Melanesia and Polynesia. Since they could not be found inland, shells were considered very valuable, and were handed down from one generation to the next. Some shells show engravings of dogs or tigers, though the origin of the tiger design remains a mystery, for this animal is not found in Borneo.

Higher up the Baram River, about 3,000 feet above sea level, live the Kelabits, a small group. Because of the inaccessability of their region, which can be reached only on foot or by plane, they have no commercial outlet for their agricultural produce.

The Muruts, who use the blowpipe, live in the Trusan Valley of Sarawak, and also in Sabah. In the last century, cholera, smallpox and malaria wiped out much of the Murut population. Today they number less than 10,000. Once a violent race of heavy drinkers, they have changed their ways since missionaries converted them to Christianity in the 1930s. In his natural state the Murut is the typical jungle man— wearing nothing more than a loin cloth, called a *chawat*, and shooting poisoned arrows from his blowpipe with uncanny skill. Except for those who have left the jungle to work on plantations, the Muruts have not been influenced by external contact, since they mainly inhabit the inaccessible country of the interior.

The Penans, masters of the blowpipe, are a small wandering tribe. Like the Kukukuku in New Guinea, they roam through the jungle, living on wild sago and other jungle crops. For all their shyness and primitive outlook they are possibly the most artistic weavers of mats in the whole region. In exchange for rubber and the gallstones of monkeys and honey-bears, they receive cloth and salt from government-subsidized trading centres. Gall stones and bladders are prized by the Chinese for medicinal use.

The coastal people are called the Melanaus: they are fairer than the Malays, and have much in common culturally with the Muruts, Kayans and Kenyahs—all belong to a group known as the Kalimantans. Some have been converted to Christianity, others, called Likos (river people) are still pagan. The Melanaus travel in large roomy boats called *Barongs*.

In northern Sarawak live the Kedayans, closely allied to the Kedayans of Brunei and Sabah, and probably of Javanese origin.

Apart from these groups Sarawak is populated by Malays, Chinese, Indians and Pakistanis. The Malay people originally came from the Malayan peninsula, Sumatra and Java. The Chinese arrived from many parts of China, but mainly from the south. Traders came at the time of the Tung Dynasty in the 7th century, and large migrations occurred when the first White Rajah, James Brooke, established himself in the 19th century in Sarawak. These were the Hokkiens, the Hakkas, who mined gold at Bau, and later the Teochews, Cantonese, Hylams and Foochows. Today the Chinese make up about one-third of the population.

Each race in Sarawak speaks a different language, but almost everyone is multi-lingual, so communications presents no problem. English is understood and widely spoken.

Native warfare: Years ago war parties and head-hunting expeditions were common-place among the Dyaks. The taking of the head *(antupala)* was considered beneficial to the people and gave the longhouse added prestige. Even today, the visitor can see

72

skulls wrapped in rattan baskets *(kelingkang)* hanging from the joists *(sadau)* of the attic. These heads are only to be found in non-Christian houses, for when missionaries convert the native peoples to Christianity the old skulls are removed and buried.

The belligerent Ibans often joined the Malays on raids, robbing and taking heads; for years they raided the Land Dyaks, who retaliated by taking Iban heads. These frequent attacks were one of the reasons for communal living. The houses were raised on stilts and when all the members were safe inside the ladders could be hauled in.

The Land Dyaks kept the heads of their enemies, and each year celebrated the festivals of the skulls. This festival lasted for seven days, and nights, with much dancing and drinking of tuak, a home-made wine. These people believed that if they did not celebrate the taking of the skulls, evil spirits might return to harm them.

The blowpipe *(sumpitan)* used by several jungle peoples shoots a noiseless dart made of hardwood, its tip coated with a poison from the sap of the Ipoh tree *(Antiaris toxicaria)*. According to legend, the Ipoh poison was discovered hundreds of years ago, when a Land Dyak in the far interior overheard a conversation among evil spirits. The number of bones found round an Ipoh tree showed how many animals died from its poison, and therefore indicated the potence of the sap.

When first taken from the tree the sap has a milky colour and consistency. After boiling for about two hours with other ingredients it changes to a dark brown and thickens. Before setting too hard it is rolled into strips and placed in leaves until required for use. When the time comes for smearing the darts the poison is removed from the leaves, moistened with the sap of the Gambier leaf and worked with pestle and mortar.

The blowpipe is about eight feet long, made from hollowed-out hardwood with an extremely smooth bore. The poisoned dart is placed in the blowpipe and projected by the force of the man's breath as he puffs into the pipe. The blower can shoot accurately over a distance of about 100 feet.

THE LONGHOUSE

Found all over Borneo, longhouses accommodate several families under the one roof. They vary considerably in size—some have only about five or six rooms, others as many as 120. Each room is occupied by a family, who use it for cooking, eating and sleeping. A large hall or verandah, about 18 feet wide, serves as a work and recreation area for all the families of the longhouse; here, women can be seen making baskets of bamboo, weaving beads or pounding padi.

Most of the longhouses are made of belian or ironwood roofed with palm leaves, and are therefore inflammable. Padi fields owned by the village surround the longhouse area, and each family has a certain part of the field for cultivation. The boundaries laid in the fields are strictly maintained, and the Dyaks believe that evil spirits will trouble a trespasser.

But the longhouses are fewer than they were, and perhaps will soon disappear. The idea of pulling them down is part of a government health campaign to help eradicate infectious diseases—a hazard to such close-knit groups. Each family will be given a cottage with a garden and fence round it—though the idea does not appeal to the Land Dyaks, who have always believed in community living.

Sabah

THE LAND BELOW THE WIND

Sabah covers an area of 29,388 square miles between five and seven degrees north on the north-east tip of Borneo, surrounded by the South China Sea to the north-west, the Sulu Sea to the north, and the Celebes Sea to the east. Labuan, an island at the entrance to Brunei Bay, forms part of Sabah.

The early pirates called Sabah *the land below the wind*, for it lay south of the typhoon region. They found shelter there when sailing became rough round the Philippines and the Sulu Archipelago.

Some say the name Sabah is derived from *Sheba*, the biblical name given to an area of southern Arabia. Sheba was on the old trade route between India and Arabia and travellers from that region calling at Borneo in search of trade, could have named Sabah in those times.

Whatever the origin of the name, Sabah is a little-known haven of beauty— just a short trip from Singapore, Kuala Lumpur or Hong Kong. The Kadazans and their dances are a few miles from the capital, Kota Kinabalu; so are the Bajaus, at work in the padi fields or rounding up their cattle on horseback. Farther inland you can see the Muruts, who still use the blow-pipe.

In wildlife sanctuaries, monkeys, orang utans and elephants can all be seen in their natural state. The Mount Kinabalu National Park covers an area of 275 square miles, and dominating it is Mount Kinabalu, the highest mountain in South-east Asia—and higher than Mount Fujiyama. If you are energetic you can climb 13,455 feet to the summit: there are specially made paths, and rest houses have been built along the way. Sabah is one of the few countries where you can see tropical rainforest and sub-alpine country in one day.

Kota Kinabalu, capital of Sabah: When I arrived in Kota Kinabalu by Malaysia-Singapore Airlines I went to the Hotel Borneo, a well-appointed hotel surrounded by large grounds with the beach on one side and the airport on the other.

Driving into the city I was impressed by the brilliant green of the grass, and the clear air, and also by the good-looking Kadazan women dressed in long black skirts with scarves tied round their heads and large straw hats. I watched them cutting grass along the roadsides, swinging their scythes in slow rhythm.

Kota Kinabalu was formerly called Jesselton, after Sir Charles Jessel, Chairman of the British North Borneo Company. Some people still use the old name. This is a modern town with about 30,000 inhabitants. Multi-storey buildings crowd the skyline, and the atmosphere is brisk and business-like. The streets roar with the noise of traffic and incessant blowing of horns, yet the charm of the tropics is still there—and the buzz of high-pitched voices bargaining in Malay, Chinese, or Kadazan. The change from one language to another is sometimes so abrupt that for a time the visitor does not realize that another language is being spoken. Most people speak several languages and English is understood everywhere.

Towards evening I climbed to the top of the hill above the city and looked out over the South China Sea. Beyond the waters of the bay I could see the islands of Sapangar to the right, Gaya ahead, and away to the left the three little islands of Sulug, Sapi and Manukan. I was reminded of a story told about Manukan—of how, in World War II, the Japanese executed all the men on the island with the exception of one, who escaped. After the Japanese had left the island, the refugee returned—to live happily with an all-female population.

Gaya Island was a settlement of the North Borneo Company in 1897. Its coral reefs and beautiful beaches are a delight for the explorer of quiet places.

Below my vantage point the traffic of the town passed steadily; across the bay the blues changed to red and gold under the rays of the setting sun. Then the lights of the town came on. In the afterglow of the short tropical sunset the scene was silent, and the smell of incense and spices rose from the plain.

The hill fort, Kota Belud: From Kota Kinabalu I travelled out to Kota Belud, home of the Bajau horsemen, 48 miles away. *Kota Belud* is a Malay name meaning hill fort. From here can be seen the magnificent Mount Kinabalu.

I found the market place aglow with the brightest fruits of the tropics—red rambutans, yellow pomelos and papayas, purple mangosteens, green oranges and yellow bananas—and the air filled with the sweet-sour smell of the durian. The crowing of fighting cocks could be heard here above the bells and cries of sellers carrying pink and green jellies, or boiled rice wrapped in a banana leaf. Some sell tobacco, roasted peanuts, boiled eggs, or slices of pineapple.

I could easily pick out the Bajau horsemen among the crowd by their embroidered jackets, turbans and black silk trousers. Not all ride with stirrups—some poke their big toes through a piece of rope hung from the saddle. They carry lances, and bells tied round the horses' necks jingle as they ride.

The island of Labuan: As early as the 7th century ships from China traded with this little island, just north of Brunei. The Dutch and Portuguese knew of Labuan (a Malay word meaning anchorage). The mariners Sir Francis Drake and Captain Kidd probably knew of it too. The island was ceded to the British by the Sultan of Brunei in 1847, and now belongs to Sabah. Men of the Royal Navy who lost their lives fighting the pirates of Borneo were buried here—so were many who died fighting the Japanese in World War II.

The 20th century visitor finds Labuan on his journey from Brunei to Sabah. A transhipment centre for cargo between the two countries, its 35 square miles produce rice, coconuts, copra, rubber and sago, as well as livestock. The main town is Victoria.

Sandakan, and other towns of the east coast: Round the coast to the east of Kota Kinabalu lies Sandakan, the trade centre of Sabah. This town has been known to the people of Mindanao and China for centuries. Once wholly a pirate port, it is still the haunt of the sea gypsies plying between the Philippines and Sabah, and some goods can be bought here cheaper than anywhere else in the world.

Sandakan was a bombed ruin at the end of World War II, but has been rebuilt to become a thriving commercial centre, and a city of beauty, surrounded by green hills clad in casuarina and flamboyants. A misty haze hangs over the town and over the harbour, where dozens of Chinese junks and larger vessels lie at anchor.

Berhala Island, two miles out, has a range of steep, multi-coloured hills that fall away to flat country on the far side. From the air these hills appear reddish in bright contrast to the blue waters. Berhala is an island for swimmers, fishing parties and sightseers.

The town of Karamunting and the Batu Sipi (buffalo rock) can be reached by outboard canoe in about half an hour. The amorphous Batu Sipi, about 30 feet high; consists of three natural pillars supporting a huge upper rock—looking something like a buffalo.

76

These Chinese were working on a construction site in Singapore. Many of the workers in building construction and road work are Sam Sui women who devote their life to manual labour

Chinese children burning "devil money". According to their belief ancestors use the money in heaven

Chinese children, in fact all children in this part of the world, help in the home and in their parents' business from an early age

Many people travelled up the Malacca River in West Malaysia: the Ming Admiral, Cheng Ho in 1409, the Portuguese in 1509, the Dutch in 1641, and the British in 1795

A tombstone in the church of St Paul in Malacca. It reads: "Hereunder lies buried Reynierd Dieu, in his life, head buyer, in service East Indies Company. Died 7th July 1655."

HIER ONDER LEYT
BEGRAVEN REY
NIERD DIEU IN
SYN LEVEN OPPER
COOPMAN IN DIENST
DER E COMP OVER
LEDEN DEN 7 IULY
Aᵒ 1655

Malacca in West Malaysia, with the government offices on the left, built by the Dutch on Portuguese foundations, the Dutch clock tower, and the British memorial. Malacca has figured in the history of the Malayan peninsula since the 8th century

Parliament House in Kuala Lumpur, Malaysia's capital city. The Malaysian House of Representatives has 144 elected members and a Senate of 60 members. The building stands 250 feet above the beautiful Lake Gardens

Malacca in West Malaysia, with the government offices on the left, built by the Dutch on Portuguese foundations, the Dutch clock tower, and the British memorial. Malacca has figured in the history of the Malayan peninsula since the 8th century

Parliament House in Kuala Lumpur, Malaysia's capital city. The Malaysian House of Representatives has 144 elected members and a Senate of 60 members. The building stands 250 feet above the beautiful Lake Gardens

HIER·ONDER·LEYT
BEGRAVEN·REYS
NIER·D·DIEŪ·IN·
SYN·LEVEN·OPPER
COOPMAN·IN·DIENST
DER·E·COMP°·OVER·
LEDEN·DEN·9·IULY·
A°·1655·

The imposing railway station at Kuala Lumpur, of Moorish architecture

School children performing in the massive Merdeka stadium at Kuala Lumpur. Each year on Merdeka day, August 31st, thousands of children parade in this stadium that holds 30,000 people

Mid-day in Kuala Lumpur or, as it is commonly known, K.L. The Capital gets its name from two rivers that meet in the city, the Klang, and the Gombak. Kuala means mouth, and Lumpur, means muddy

The waterfront at Penang's main town, Georgetown, once the pride of the British East India Company

Trishaws are common in South-east Asia. The fares are about the same as for taxis, but you see more. The drivers sleep in them when work is finished

Dental nurses at Penang Dental Hospital. Over 50% of Malaysia's population is under 18 years. These nurses are trained to perform preventative and curative work on children 12 years old and under

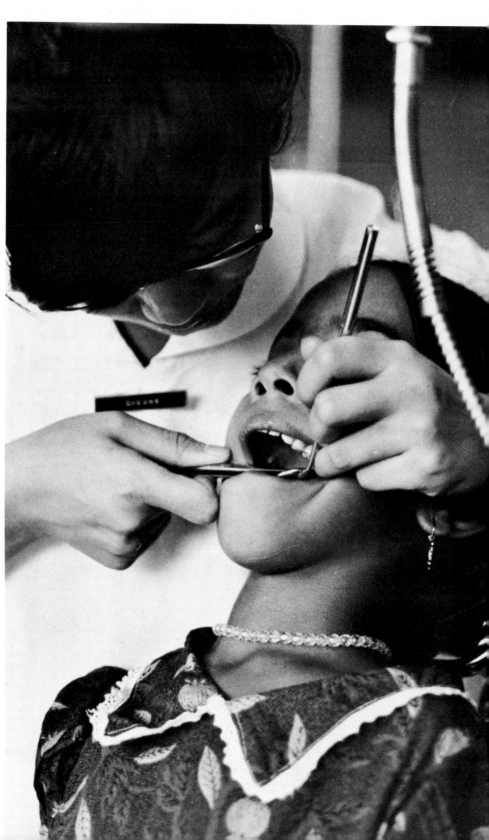

The snake temple at Sungei Kluang on Penang island. The temple has dozens of snakes inside, and they are fed by devotees who leave eggs and other food

Noodles drying in the sun at Georgetown, Penang

Latex dripping from a rubber tree in Malaysia

At Sungei Jaong on the Sarawak River in Borneo, a rock carving was found buried in the mud, and its age is said to be about 1000 years, but no one knows for certain. From 700 A.D. to 1550 Sungei Jaong was a trading station used by Chinese merchants travelling between China and Borneo

The Gomanton Caves, about ten miles south of the Sandakan harbour, contain relics of mesolithic origin. Inside two of these caves, set in the 700-foot Gomanton Hill, swiftlets build their famous nests. Another cave is occupied by hundreds of bats: at night, they fly out in one stream that lasts about half an hour.

Farther round the coast near the border of Kalimantan, is the residency of Tawau. You can fly there from Sandakan. Tawau, Sabah's third largest town, has a thriving economy. It is an agricultural centre producing hemp, copra, cocoa, timber, rubber, tobacco and palm oil. Its wealth has attracted people from the Philippines, Timor, Indonesia and the Celebes for many years. People of many races walk its streets to buy or barter in the stores. The small boats in Cowie harbour here are laden with produce to be traded for manufactured articles and food from abroad.

Across Darvel Bay, to the north of Tawau, is Lahad Datu, one of the earliest trading stations of the North Borneo Company. An isolated place, its waters are populated by the Sulus, who live on their boats. The sea gypsies, too, live and die on their vessels—I saw them in Sabah, as I had earlier at Zamboanga on the island of Mindanao in the Philippines.

The town of Semporna (a Malay word meaning perfection) lies at the southern tip of Darvel Bay, with the island of Bum Bum shielding it. At most times a peaceful place, Semporna has seen moments of violence. In 1954 a pirate raid brought death to many Europeans and natives, with the doss of about $M200,000 worth of merchandise. The pirates came from the Philippines, and have made several small raids on the town since. In 1963, 36 people were convicted of piracy. The Philippines have naval patrols in the Sulu Sea keeping constant watch for pirates and smugglers.

PEOPLES OF SABAH

The native people of Sabah make up about 70% of the population, which totals over 500,000. Kadazans comprise the largest group, followed by the Bajaus and the Muruts. Other peoples, some from the Philippines, make up smaller groups. The rest of the population is Chinese, Indian, and European.

Most people live along the west coast, for much of the interior is covered with impenetrable jungle. Along the sparsely populated east coast, for the first 150 miles of the Kinabatangan River, the people are Muslim—their beliefs introduced mainly by visiting traders from Brunei, Indonesia and the Malay Archipelago long ago. Farther up the Kinabatangan River, inland, the natives are either pagan or Christian. Missionaries of all Christian denominations have established themselves in the country.

The most progressive of Sabah's peoples, the Kadazans, inhabit the west coast and the plains of the interior. Once they were headhunters: today they are a stable community of agriculturalists, with a keen interest in education and the progress of their country. They have their own language, music and culture. Originally, they lived at Tambunan and Keningau in the interior. Keningau is still a centre for Kadazans, though Muruts live there as well.

Stocky and small in stature, and relatively light-skinned, the Kadazans have a long association with the Chinese. The children of mixed marriages are usually brought up as Chinese.

Kadazan women are hard workers, spending long hours in the padis, planting rice with bent backs, or repairing banks. Like other tribes, the Kadazans celebrate the harvest with wine—theirs is tapai, a potent rice wine. The women dress for the occasion in black velvet and lace, ornamented with gold and silver coins.

The Bajaus live along the coastal fringes. These people have played a significant part in the history of Sabah. In 1896 Mat Salleh and his Bajau followers from the many rivers attacked the headquarters of the British North Borneo Company, and resisted their rule for some time. The rivers had been under the rule of the Sultan of Brunei until 1899 and were called "independent rivers", for the people who lived along them controlled the waterways. In 1899 the Company purchased all the land and rivers from the Sultan and so they ceased to be independent. Mat Salleh fought his last fight at Teboh in 1900. He had retreated from the coast into the interior and built a large fort to repel the opposing forces, but his efforts proved ineffective when pitted against the Company's cannon.

Like the Bajaus, the Sulus, Binadans and Ilanuns came from the Philippines to settle on the coast. These tribes once formed the band of pirates that ravaged the seas round Borneo and the Sulu Archipelago, plundering the coastal villages. Today they are farmers and fishermen.

It is believed that the Chinese first settled in Borneo in the Sung dynasty (960–1279 A.D.), when a revival in painting, porcelain making and printing led to the promotion of foreign trade. The Chinese were skilled navigators, and contacts with other countries began to increase at this time. A Chinese settlement on the Kinabatangan River dates back to the 14th century.

Many Chinese came to Borneo in the late 19th century as agriculturalists and traders. People from Shantung and Hakka were offered ten-acre plots of land. The Shantung people's early attempts at cultivation were not very successful, for they were better craftsmen than agriculturalists. They sold brooms, hats and bags to supplement their income, but before long they learnt to cultivate their plots well too. The Hakkas had been farmers for generations, and as such contributed much to the growth and development of Sabah.

THE SABAH GOVERNMENT—PLANS FOR DEVELOPMENT

Sabah is governed by two constitutions, Federal and State, and in Kuala Lumpur, is represented by 16 members in the Malaysian House of Representatives and three Senators. The Malaysian constitution provides for a large degree of autonomy for Sabah, including State control of immigration, freedom of religion, and the continued use of English as the official language for a period of ten years.

The Head of State is appointed by the Yang di-Pertuan Agong. The State Cabinet consists of the Chief Minister and eight other ministers; and the Legislative Assembly has a speaker, 32 elected members and five nominated members.

Local government is carried out in the main towns and districts by councils and boards responsible for their own finances and affairs. Members of the town boards are elected or appointed by the Minister for Local Government.

Under a community development plan, millions of dollars are being spent on schemes that will make Sabah one of the most progressive countries in South-east Asia. Much emphasis has been placed on road construction, the main project being the $M25,000,000 east-west highway linking Sandakan with Kota Kinabalu. This is a joint venture between Australia and Sabah. Australia has contributed over $M14,000,000, as well as engineers to supervise the project.

The Government has health clinics in each village throughout the country, and plans to build more hospitals. A flying doctor service, called the Rural Air Service, brings medical help to the more remote and inaccessible areas. When the situation warrants, the Royal Malaysian Air Force works in conjunction with the Rural Air Service.

In Sabah, education is considered of great importance. The establishment of more primary and secondary schools and free education at primary level will benefit children of all races. Two teacher training colleges provide courses in English, Chinese and Malay, and plan to increase their intake of student teachers, since many teachers in Sabah are still untrained. Special emphasis has been placed on technical education, and new technical colleges are being built to cope with the growing need.

Sabah's economy relies on the export of timber and rubber. Forest reserves cover nearly ten thousand square miles. Most of the rubber grows on the west coast and interior plains. Plantations cover 250,000 acres, 50% of which are high yielding. Crops other than rubber have been developed to increase the stability of the country's economy. Coconut, manila hemp, cocoa and oil palm plantations have been extended in past years. The volume of trade (carried on mainly with Hong Kong and Singapore) shows a steady increase. Rice is grown for local use, as wet padi, dry hill padi and also in rotation with other crops. Irrigation works, resettlement schemes and improved communications will help to boost the agricultural output.

Brunei is a beautiful little principality of 2,226 square miles between Sarawak and Sabah, and one of the wealthiest areas in South-east Asia. Some 100,000 people live in this Islamic Sultanate, which forms two enclaves separated by the Limbang Valley of Sarawak.

There is no direct route by air into Brunei from West Malaysia; you enter either from Sarawak in the south or from Sabah in the north.

The Sultanate of Brunei

ONCE A HOTBED OF PIRATES

The earliest trade known in Brunei was carried out with China, in junks—the slow, flat-bottomed Chinese trading boats.

Hindu influence spread to the State in the reign of the Majapahit Empire in Java, when Javanese repelled Sulu pirates from Brunei in 1368. Brunei is one of the countries mentioned in Javanese records as being conquered in the reign of the last King of Majapahit, Angka Wijaya. According to the translation of a historical tablet in Brunei, the first ruler, who introduced Islam to Brunei, was Sultan Mohammed with his brother Sultan Akhmed. He had a daughter from his marriage to the sister of the Chinese Raja. She married Sheriff Ali, who was an Arab, and who took the name Sultan Berkat. Sheriff Ali was descended from the Amir of the faithful Hasan, the grandson of the messenger of God. The Bruneis claim descent from the legendary Besiong, and there was a close relationship with Johore on the Malayan peninsula.

From the 15th century Brunei's wealth began to grow. Trade with China flourished and embassies were established in Peking.

The Malay nobles began their reign by imposing taxes, selling Dyaks as slaves or consigning them to forced labour. In the 16th century after the Portuguese had occupied Malacca, many traders fled to Brunei, further adding to its economic strength. Brunei became known as a centre for stolen goods, where the nobles were in league with the pirates, who came from such places as Mindanao. Eventually, traders and merchant ships refused to call at Brunei. Piracy continued right up until the 19th century, when the White Rajah of Sarawak, Sir James Brooke, and the British Navy made a concerted effort to quell it. In 1846 the island of Labuan was ceded to Britain as a base for anti-piracy measures. The following year, the Sultan

96

COLOUR

*Cloisters of the Omar Ali Saifuddin Mosque
at Brunei*

Burning gas at the Seria oilfields in Brunei

General store in Brunei, with stock of everything from tombstones to kitchen-ware

Malay girls dance in Singapore

entered into a treaty with Britain for the promotion of trade relations and the mutual suppression of piracy.

In 1888 Brunei came under the protection of Great Britain, and a British Resident did much to establish law and order between 1906 and 1941. Roads were built, people were encouraged to become farmers and fishermen, housing was improved and trade flourished. The discovery of the oilfield in 1929 meant growing prosperity.

When the Japanese occupied Brunei in December 1941, trade came to a standstill. Labour was forced, and crops harvested were used to feed the invading forces. Starvation and disease prevailed among the indigenous peoples.

In 1945 the Allied forces landed, and set about repairing the damage done by the Japanese. W. J. Peel became Resident in July 1946 when the British Military Administration transferred power to the Civil Administration.

TODAY A SULTANATE UNDER BRITISH PROTECTION

A treaty concluded with the United Kingdom in 1959 abolished the post of British Resident and made Brunei internally self-governing. The British Government remains responsible for defence and external affairs, paying over a million pounds a year towards the upkeep of a battalion of Gurkhas stationed there.

Supreme administrative authority is vested in the Sultan. Hassanal Bolkiah Mu'izaddin Waddaulah became the 29th Sultan of Brunei when his father, Sir Omar Ali Saifuddin abdicated voluntarily in 1968. The Sultan, a Sandhurst graduate and devout Muslim, mixes freely with his people and takes an active interest in the affairs of the community. It was his father and predecessor who may be regarded as the architect of modern Brunei, who introduced parliamentary procedures, new social services, and development in commerce and industry.

The Brunei Constitution of 1959 provided for the establishment of five councils: a Legislative Council, a Council of Ministers, a Religious Council, a Privy Council, and a Council of Succession. Judicial power is held by a High Court and a Court of Appeal presided over by a Chief Justice.

The Legislative Council comprises 21 members—all Brunei citizens. Ten are elected into office directly, six—including the State Secretary and Attorney General and State Financial Officer—are ex-officio members, and five are appointed by the Sultan on nomination. The Council exercises financial control and debates Government actions. It holds public meetings, presided over by a speaker, at the Royal Lapau, the new Assembly Hall in the centre of Brunei Town, built at a cost of over $B8,000,000.

The Sultan presides over the Council of Ministers, which deals with all matters of policy. The eleven members—six ex-officio, four unofficial (who are also members of the Legislative Council) and the High Commissioner—meet privately.

The British High Commissioner advises the Sultan on all matters except those concerning the Muslim faith, for which the Religious Council is responsible. Its 16 members are appointed by the Sultan and presided over by the State Religious Affairs Officer.

The Sultan presides over the Privy Council, consisting of six ex-officio members, the High Commissioner, the Regents, and any other persons the Sultan wishes to appoint.

Succession to the throne is determined by the Council of Succession. Its members, called *Cheterias*, are taken from the Legislative and Religious councils.

The Sultanate is divided into four administrative districts: Brunei and Muara, Temburong, Tutong and Belait. Each district has its local council, the majority of members being elected by universal suffrage. District Officers are advised by their council on local matters. In addition, each group of villages has a *Mukim* council—whose members—prominent residents of the villages—are appointed by the Government. This council helps the District Officer look after the welfare of the villages.

The capital of Brunei is set in a wide sweep of river. Its houses are grouped together in small villages, some connected by precarious bridges. In the city centre, new buildings are gradually replacing the old. One of Brunei's most outstanding buildings, the Omar Ali Saifuddin Mosque, completed in 1958, was built on land reclaimed from the Kedayan River, a branch of the Brunei River, at a cost of $B8,000,000. The Sultan after whom it was named desired that it be built as a monument to the country's Islamic faith. Huge white pillars, marble floors and stained glass windows give the mosque a remarkable grandeur, and its gold dome dominates the city.

Brunei Town is small, and quieter than the other cities of the region. It has no heavy traffic or bustle. The sounds I heard as I strolled along the main street (often drowned in Singapore or Kuala Lumpur) were the excited babble of Chinese, the bang of an occasional firecracker, the shuffling of feet of the passing parade of Muslims on their way to the mosque, the chatter and laughter of school children, and the barking and yelping of dogs.

More than half of the town's 10,000 people live in the Kampong Ayer (water village)—a group of about 30 small villages built over the water. Water "roads" bisecting the blocks of houses perched on stilts make it a kind of tropical Venice, with a continual stream of boat traffic moving to and from the mainland and in and out between the houses. Sellers of fruit, vegetables and clothing travel the waterways in outboard canoes; children play on the verandahs, or swim in the water, when not at school or sailing to school in small rakish boats.

The houses are made of timber with galvanized iron roofs. Some are two-storeyed and quite lavishly furnished. Aerials can be seen above many roofs, for Brunei has its own radio station. Water and electricity are connected to the houses from the mainland.

Traditionally, the people of the village were weavers and silversmiths, fishermen, traders and pirates: today, large numbers work in offices and Government departments.

The Government has attempted, more than once, to shift the village onto the mainland, but the plan has not found the support of Malays, who are very attached to their tradition of living on water. The most recent resettlement scheme has been more successful, for land grants and housing loans have provided the villagers with more incentive to leave the cramped conditions of the water village.

The State's main source of income is oil which comes from off-shore and shore wells at Seria, a few miles to the south of Brunei Town. Oil was struck here in 1929, and today Brunei is the second largest oil producer in the British Commonwealth.

A visit to the oilfields by bus or taxi makes a fascinating and inexpensive trip. A bitumen road connects Brunei Town with Seria, but you travel by boat through Kampong Ayer, past the houses on stilts. The smell of oil is strong for the newcomer.

That Seria is the busiest place in Brunei is not surprising when one considers that the Government receives $U.S.14,000,000 in income tax from the oil company, and $8,500,000 a year in royalties. With the off-shore fields at Ampa, the output has increased to 119,000 barrels a day, drawn from 420 wells. The oil is pumped to Lutong, the refining town in Sarawak, where it is shipped by tankers for export. A power station built in the oilfield area provides cheap power for industrial and domestic use.

Oil makes Brunei one of the wealthiest places in South-east Asia. Fishing, forestry and rubber aid the economy to a lesser extent, and until recently, agriculture was restricted to internal requirements. Brunei silversmiths are renowned for their skills. Most of their silverware is sold locally—the Sultan being the main customer.

The two ports of the country, Brunei Town and Kuala Belait, are trade centres. A very favourable balance of trade has been maintained: exports sometimes amount to four times as much as imports. Apart from crude oil, exports include rubber, timber, jelutong, sago, rice, pepper, livestock and cutch, a bark extract from the mangrove. Imported goods include food, tobacco, textiles, clothing, chemicals, machinery, petroleum products and building materials.

PROGRESS AND DEVELOPMENT

The Government of Brunei has extensive plans for future development. One of their major projects is the establishment of a deep-water port at Muara, where the Pelompong Spit provides a natural breakwater. Ships will have access to the mainland through a two-and-a-quarter-mile channel, to be cut out of the spit. When completed, the port at Muara will have facilities comparable with those found in any of the world's large harbours.

The new airport, planned for Berakas near Brunei Town, is another project that will significantly improve the country's transport and communications and consequently increase trade and capital investment. At the moment, Brunei cannot be reached by air except by way of internal flights from Sarawak or Sabah. The 12,000-foot runway of the new airport will be safe for any heavy aircraft, and the best equipment will be provided for the functioning of a large, international airport.

The Government's National Development Plan is also aimed at diversifying the economy, to make it less dependent on the oil industry. Agriculture and forestry are becoming more important as drainage and irrigation systems improve, and more arable land is found. Research stations and training schools for farmers have been set up to promote agricultural development. Better breeds of cattle will help the livestock industry.

The citizens of Brunei already enjoy a standard of living that is one of the highest in South-east Asia. Unemployment is not known—the average income is about $B1,400 a year. The Government imposes no income tax on salaries and wages; health, housing and education schemes are available to the public, and the man who drives a car (purchased on an interest-free loan) pays only 20 Brunei cents a gallon for his petrol.

Those living in remote areas are no longer cut off from civilization. The Government subsidizes the purchase of transistor radios for the inhabitants of the more inaccessible forested areas. Outdoor clinics, travelling dispensaries and a flying doctor service bring medical and dental help to the interior.

School-children in Brunei may be instructed in one or more of three languages: Malay, Mandarin, or English. The Malay schools, both primary and secondary, are financed by the Government. English schools, ranging from kindergarten to secondary, are provided by the Government and by the missions. After six years at primary school and five at high school, students may sit for the higher school certificate; successful candidates can then obtain a scholarship from the Government, from a mission or the Brunei Shell Company, to study at a university overseas.

Under a new education scheme the Government will offer better training to skilled workers and tradesmen, and attempt to eliminate illiteracy—still prevalent among inland peoples. A larger teacher training college is under construction, and three trades and engineering schools at Brunei Town, Tutong and Kuala Belait are now equipped to give excellent courses.

103

For the traveller

Singapore and West Malaysia have a thriving tourist trade—one which is growing each year at an astonishing rate. East Malaysia and Brunei are beginning to take more part in the industry, being easily accessible by sea and by air. Qantas and other airlines call at Singapore and Kuala Lumpur where you can connect with regular domestic flights to Kuching or Kota Kinabalu.

The visitor to these countries meets with a great deal of kindness and courtesy and, if he speaks English, finds no insurmountable language barrier, for English is spoken and understood by a great many people in all the larger cities.

Entry formalities: Visitors to Singapore, Malaysia and Brunei must possess a valid passport. Visas are required by travellers from some countries if their stay in Singapore exceeds 90 hours, and in Malaysia and Brunei if their stay exceeds three months. British Commonwealth countries are among those exempted from the visa requirement.

A current health certificate of vaccination against smallpox is needed. Malaria has been wiped out in the towns, but the traveller venturing inland in northern Borneo would be advised to take precautions.

There is no restriction on the amount of money brought into these countries in the form of travellers' cheques, and an unlimited amount of foreign currency notes may be imported from all countries outside the region with the exception of India and Indonesia.

Local currency: The unit of currency used throughout the region is the dollar—the Malaysian dollar ($M), the Singapore dollar ($S) and the Brunei dollar ($B) are all of equal value and can be interchanged in each country. Three Malaysian, Brunei or Singapore dollars are approximately equal to one United States dollar. Travellers' cheques may be cashed at banks and hotels, or by licensed money-changers for a fee.

Accommodation: Singapore has many hotels, with prices ranging from $S18 and $S52 for a single air-conditioned room. I often stay at the Goodwood Park—its atmosphere is homely and the service excellent. I can also recommend the Gordon Grill for its superb and inexpensive food, served by tiny Chinese waitresses.

Air-conditioned hotels, hostels and rest houses are plentiful all over West Malaysia. Prices range from $M5 to $M60 for a single room. In Kuala Lumpur I stayed at the Federal Hotel.

In Sarawak and Sabah single rooms in hotels cost between $M12 and $M30 or more. Similar accommodation in Brunei is more expensive.

Although hotels and restaurants add a ten per cent service charge to their bills, tipping is also expected.

Transport: In each country the visitor may choose between bus, taxi, trishaw and hire-car. Malaysia also has an excellent railway system.

In Sabah and Brunei the taxis have no meters, and the price of the journey is negotiated beforehand. Fares are generally reasonable, though in Kuching I was really taken for a ride. A two-hour drive to the longhouse and back, a distance of about 20 miles, cost me $M90! In Singapore and West Malaysia the basic rate gauged by the meter is 40 cents for the first mile, and 20 cents for each additional half-mile. Trishaw fares are comparable.

In Singapore a sampan will take you round the harbour for $S2.50 an hour, or you can make a longer trip to the neighbouring islands in a luxury vessel for $S10. Speedboats can be hired in East Malaysia and Brunei. The Tourist Board in each centre arranges all-day trips by bus.

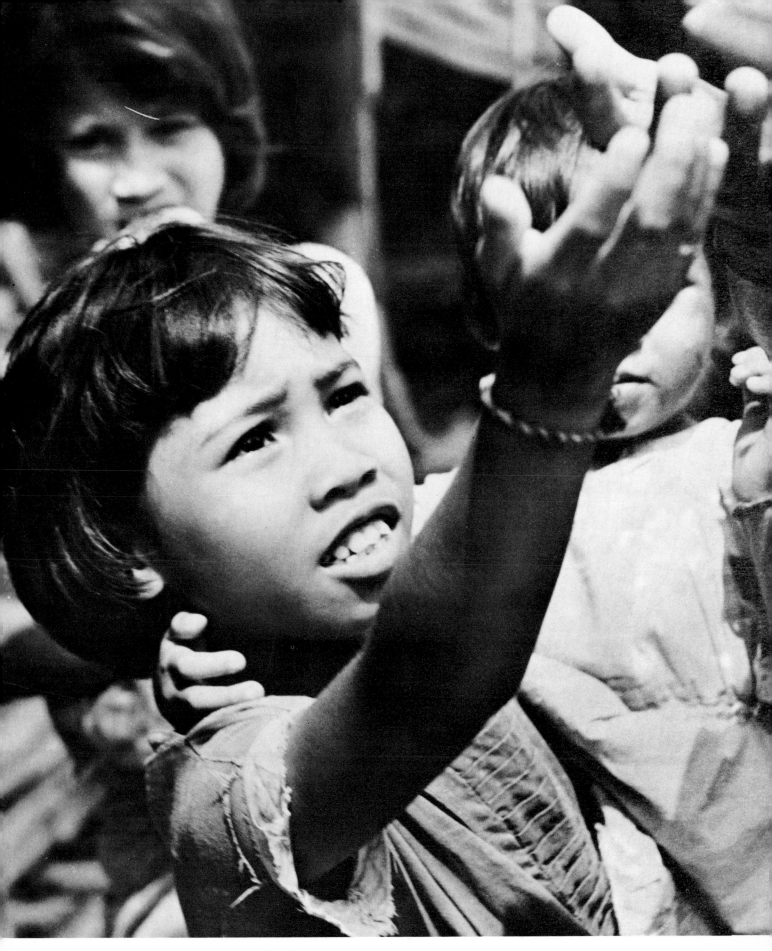

Land Dyak children in Sarawak. The Land Dyaks live in the first division of Sarawak

The sacred Lemba Bumbun pole of Sarawak.
It is decorated with sacred carvings and the
skulls of slain enemies

*Land Dyak boys of Sarawak. These Land
Dyaks number about 60,000, and plant hill
padi—rice grown on dry land*

The Land Dyaks live in long-houses, which are really whole villages. Each village lives in a long-house made up of a number of rooms

A young Kadazan girl from Sabah. The Kadazan people are the most progressive of the indigenous people of Sabah

The Kadazan women when young are recognized as being among the most beautiful in South-east Asia

The water buffalo, from India to Portuguese Timor, is an animal with many tasks. It is used in the padi fields, it pulls vehicles, and is slow yet sure to ride

Portion of Brunei Town. The Sultanate of Brunei is one of the richest States for its size in the world, gaining most of its wealth from oil

With all merging nations education is of great importance. Brunei is no exception. The majority of people in Singapore, Malaysia, and Brunei speak two or three languages

Children outside their house in the Kampong Ayer (water village) in Brunei

Kampong Ayer in the Brunei River. It is really about 30 villages joined together. Kampong Ayer shelters more than half the population of Brunei's 10,000

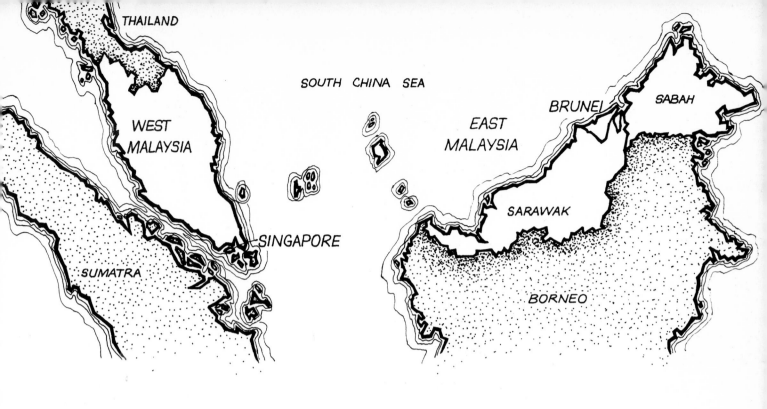

THAILAND

SOUTH CHINA SEA

WEST
MALAYSIA

EAST
MALAYSIA

BRUNEI

SABAH

SARAWAK

SINGAPORE

SUMATRA

BORNEO

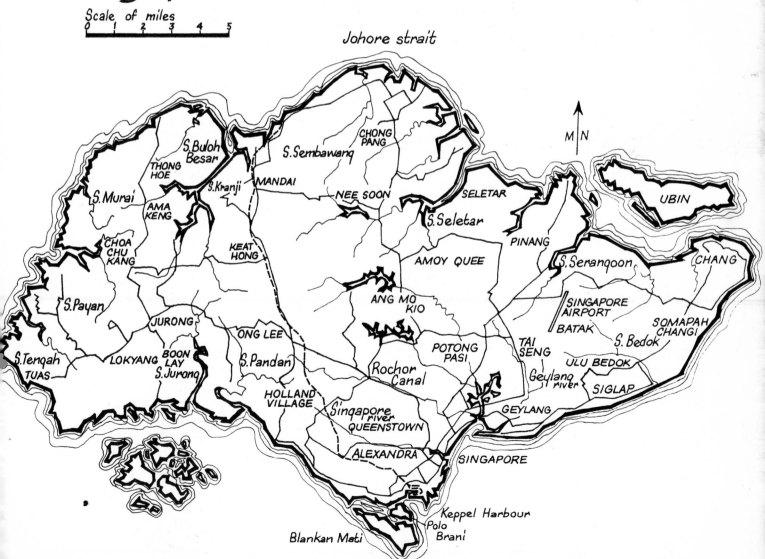

Singapore

Scale of miles
0 1 2 3 4 5

Johore strait

M N

S. Buloh
Besar

THONG
HOE

CHONG
PANG

S. Sembawang

S. Murai

S. Kranji

MANDAI

AMA
KENG

NEE SOON

SELETAR

UBIN

S. Seletar

CHOA
CHU
KANG

KEAT
HONG

PINANG

AMOY QUEE

S. Serangoon

CHANG

S. Payan

ANG MO
KIO

SINGAPORE
AIRPORT

SOMAPAH
CHANGI

JURONG

ONG LEE

BATAK

S. Bedok

S. Pandan

POTONG
PASI

TAI
SENG

ULU BEDOK

S.Tengah
TUAS

LOKYANG

BOON
LAY

S. Jurong

Rochor
Canal

Geylang
river

SIGLAP

HOLLAND
VILLAGE

Singapore
river
QUEENSTOWN

GEYLANG

ALEXANDRA

SINGAPORE

Keppel Harbour
Polo
Brani

Blankan Mati

West Malaysia

Scale of Miles

0   50   100

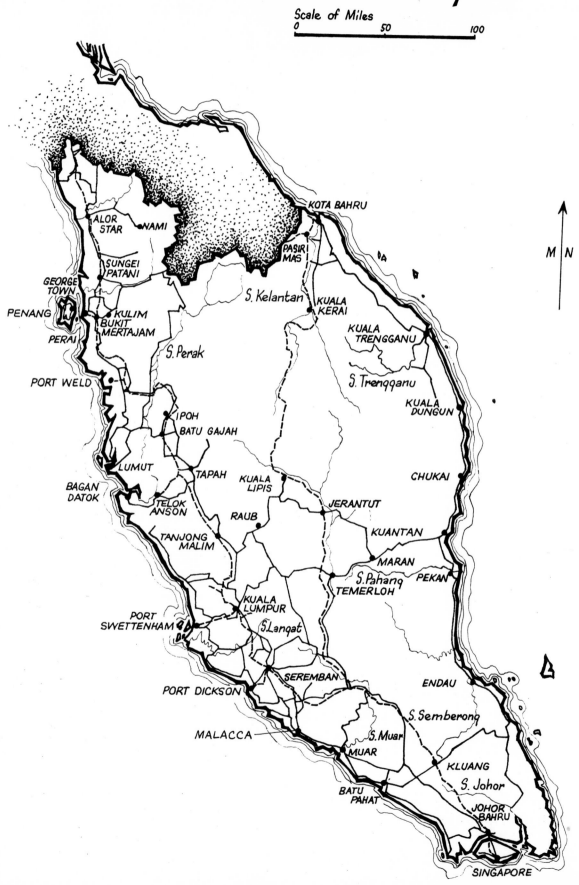

M | N

ALOR STAR

NAMI

SUNGEI PATANI

GEORGE TOWN

PENANG

KULIM
BUKIT MERTAJAM

PERAI

S. Perak

PORT WELD

IPOH

BATU GAJAH

LUMUT

TAPAH

KUALA LIPIS

BAGAN DATOK

TELOK ANSON

RAUB

TANJONG MALIM

KOTA BAHRU

PASIR MAS

S. Kelantan

KUALA KERAI

KUALA TRENGGANU

S. Trengganu

KUALA DUNGUN

CHUKAI

JERANTUT

KUANTAN

MARAN

S. Pahang

PEKAN

TEMERLOH

KUALA LUMPUR

S. Langat

PORT SWETTENHAM

SEREMBAN

ENDAU

PORT DICKSON

S. Semberong

MALACCA

S. Muar

MUAR

KLUANG

S. Johor

BATU PAHAT

JOHOR BAHRU

SINGAPORE

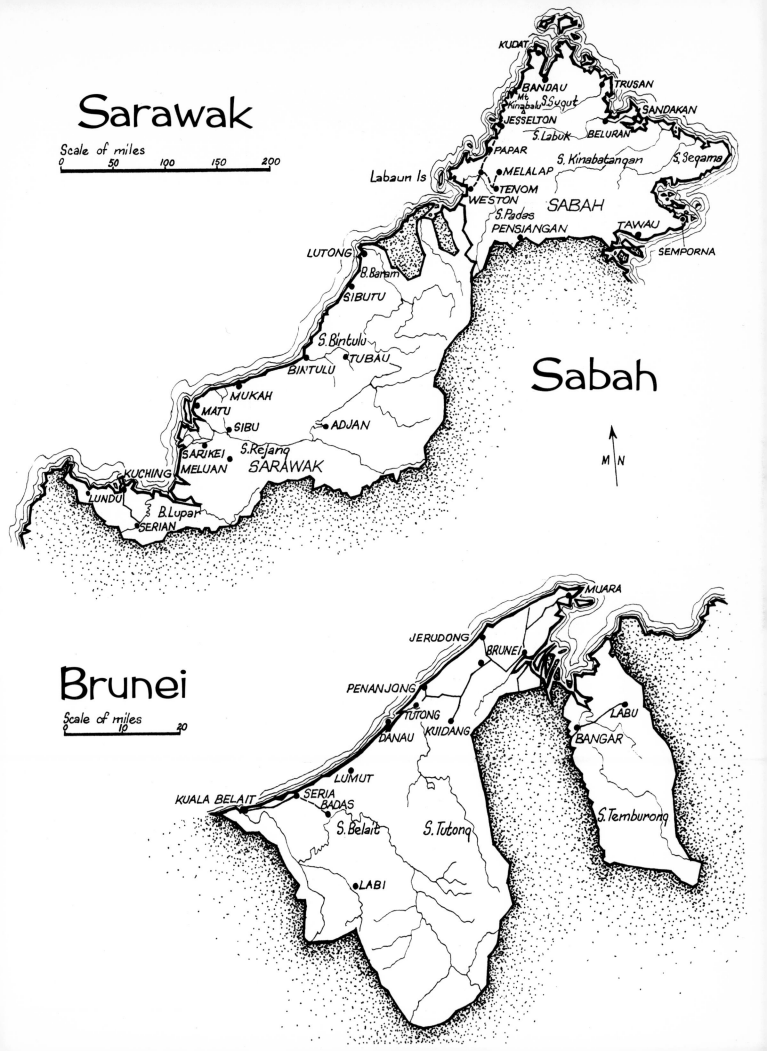

Index

Acknowledgements

The author wishes to thank these people for their help in supplying information: George Seow, First Secretary, Singapore High Commission, Canberra; S. Rajaratnam, Minister for Foreign Affairs, Government of Singapore; Li Vei Chen, Press Secretary, Singapore; Lam Peng Loon, Director, Singapore Tourist Promotion Board; Ong Choon Hay, Yu Loon Ching, Raymon Huang, Dennis Pile, Tourist Promotion Board; Wong Lee Siok Tin and Claude Doral, Radio Singapore; Dr Ho Guan Lim, Aloysius Ang Koon Wah, Cheong Soo Pieng, Seah Kim Joo, Johnnie Johnson and Pat Donoghue, Singapore; Mavis Oei and Mario Ruosch, Goodwood Park Hotel; Don Beach, *Singapore Lady;* Peter Lo, John Clark and Dora Khoo, Qantas; C. M. Wong, Secretary, Chinese Chamber of Commerce; Dr Goh Poh Seng, President, Singapore National Theatre Trust; George E. Howling, Malaysia-Singapore Airlines, Singapore; Robert Lim and Dr Wong Kong Meng, Malacca; Osman Siru, Director, Department of Tourism, Kuala Lumpur; J. M. Candlish, Second Secretary, British High Commission, Kuala Lumpur; Ralph E. Schelling, Federal Hotel, Kuala Lumpur; Lee Sim Fook, Ministry of Agriculture, Kuala Lumpur; Inche Shrom Yob, Curator, Kuala Lumpur Museum; P. O. Menon, Penang Tourist Association; Yong Cheng Wah, Penang; Dr Chellie Sundram, Dental Hospital, Penang; Lucas Chin, Sarawak Museum; Ismail Hassan and Rosalyn Sitie, Radio Sarawak, Kuching; Tan Han Boon, Chairman, Sarawak Tourist Association; Happy Low, State Secretariat, Brunei; G. de Frietes, Director, Broadcasting and Information, Brunei; John Maidment, Brunei-Shell, Seria, Brunei; Yang Berhormat Awang 'Abdul 'Aziz bin Pehin Udana Khatib Awang Haji Umar, Legislative Council, Brunei; Robert Cheng, Director, Sabah Tourist Association, Kota Kinabalu; Michael Chin, Radio Malaysia, Kota Kinabalu, Sabah; John Ulm, Alex Smyth, Dick Morris, Qantas, Sydney; Sir Charles Moses C.B.E., Asian Broadcasting Union, Sydney.